THE
MINISTER
AS MORAL
THEOLOGIAN

THE MINISTER AS MORAL THEOLOGIAN

ETHICAL DIMENSIONS OF PASTORAL LEADERSHIP

SONDRA WHEELER

Baker Academic

a division of Baker Publishing Group
Grand Rapids, Michigan

Published by Baker Academic
a division of Baker Publishing Group
P.O. Box 6287, Grand Rapids, MI 49516-6287
www.bakeracademic.com

Printed in the United States of America

Library of Congress Cataloging-in-Publication Data
Names: Wheeler, Sondra Ely, 1956– author.
Title: The minister as moral theologian : ethical dimensions of pastoral leadership / Sondra Wheeler.
Description: Grand Rapids : Baker Academic, 2017. | Includes index.
Identifiers: LCCN 2016051158 | ISBN 9780801097843 (pbk.)
Subjects: LCSH: Clergy—Professional ethics. | Christian leadership. | Professional ethics. | Christian ethics. | Pastoral theology.
Classification: LCC BV4011.5 .W44 2017 | DDC 241/.641—dc23
LC record available at https://lccn.loc.gov/2016051158

In keeping with biblical principles of creation stewardship, Baker Publishing Group advocates the responsible use of our natural resources. As a member of the Green Press Initiative, our company uses recycled paper when possible. The text paper of this book is composed in part of post-consumer waste.

17 18 19 20 21 22 23   7 6 5 4 3 2 1

To my students
over the last twenty-five years,
from whom I have learned much
of what I know about ministry

Contents

Acknowledgments

Books, even those with individual authors, are always collaborative efforts. As a writer you are in conversation with other writers, both those you know personally and those you meet only in print. For a book like this one, which draws extensively on years spent talking with students at all levels of ministry experience and on formal and informal consultations with ministers across a wide variety of traditions and settings, the sense of a collective labor is particularly strong. Whatever insight it has to offer is the fruit of a community of students, thinkers, and practitioners experimenting with the possibilities and wrestling with the perils of leading the church as a moral community. The book's dedication to the students I have taught over twenty-five years is in happy recognition of some of that debt.

A few members of the community of scholars and practitioners deserve special mention here because their long association with the author made them liable to be called upon for ideas and feedback, in response to which they were uniformly gracious and helpful. In this category belong my teaching colleagues Daniel Mejia and Joe Bush, and my onetime seminary classmate Anna Verlee Copeland, now a pastor in Maine. I also thank Tom Berlin, pastor and chairman of the board of Wesley Seminary where I teach, whose feedback and encouragement were invaluable, and Mandy Sayers, an alum of our school who is both a fine minister and a meticulous editor.

Finally, I must mention a few scholars whose work in this area has been particularly provocative and helpful to me as a thinker and teacher: Rebekah Miles, who first gave me the idea that pastors could call upon congregants to do their moral homework; Richard Gula, whose work on the professional character of ministry offered me new ways of thinking about power; and Margaret Farley, whose reflections on the sustenance or failure of human commitments continues to illuminate both my work and my life. For the wisdom and insight they have brought to our shared field, I am grateful.

Introduction

WHY THIS BOOK?

Thirty years ago, when I was in seminary, literature on the ethics of pastoral ministry was remarkably sparse. What material did exist had more to do with manners and professional etiquette than with the moral problems that arise in ministry, and offered little in the way of tools for analysis or standards for judgment. Gaylord Noyce, longtime professor of pastoral theology at Yale Divinity School, was among the first to address this problem with his 1988 book *Pastoral Ethics*.[1] In this work, he used the then-developing field of professional ethics to provide a framework for reflecting on the responsibilities of clergy.

In the decades since, many other writers have turned their attention to this topic. Recent books in the field are numerous, and many offer sound judgment and good practical advice. Among the general texts I have found useful in my many years of seminary teaching are Rebekah Miles's *The Pastor as Moral Guide*, William Willimon's *Calling and Character*, Joe Trull and James Carter's *Ministerial Ethics*, Richard Gula's *Ethics in Pastoral Ministry*

---

1. Gaylord Noyce, *Pastoral Ethics: Professional Responsibilities of the Clergy* (Nashville: Abingdon, 1988).

and his more recent *Just Ministry*, Joseph Bush's *Gentle Shepherding*, and Barbara Blodgett's *Lives Entrusted*.[2] These books provide various sorts of help, whether as broad moral and theological resources for understanding the particular ministry of the ordained or as carefully developed arguments for the nature of moral obligations in ministry. Some offer detailed accounts of what is at stake and what harm is done when professional norms are violated. Others enter into particular debates about the duties of confidentiality and their limits, the possibilities and risks of friendship between pastors and congregants, and the challenges of balancing professional obligations with personal and family life.

In addition, there is an emerging literature focused more narrowly on pastoral sexual misconduct, its patterns, its effects, and appropriate responses to it. Beginning with the seminal work of Marie Fortune,[3] these themes are followed up in works like Stanley Grenz and Roy Bell's *Betrayal of Trust*.[4] Other relevant works could also be cited, including a number of denominational statements. Most of these texts offer analyses of why such misconduct is so serious and so destructive along with practical guidance and strategies for establishing and maintaining necessary boundaries, and all articulate clear standards of conduct.

Given all of this it is reasonable to ask, Why another book on this subject? My answer to this sensible question is twofold. First, I am interested in calling attention to all the dimensions of pastoral ministry that involve ministers deeply in work we normally assign to the province of Christian ethics. This is not simply a matter of a particular clergyperson's intellectual interests or preferences. The ordinary practice of ministry *requires* pastors to serve as moral theologians within their congregations. It is demanded by the

2. For more on these and other recommended books, see the further reading section at the back of the present volume.

3. Marie Fortune, *Is Nothing Sacred? When Sex Invades the Pastoral Relationship* (San Francisco: Harper, 1989).

4. Stanley J. Grenz and Roy D. Bell, *Betrayal of Trust: Confronting and Preventing Clergy Sexual Misconduct*, 2nd ed. (Grand Rapids: Baker Books, 2001).

nature of their regular work as preachers and teachers and givers of counsel as well as by the role they inhabit as visible leaders of communities of faith. In fact, pastors will be teaching ethics, whether consciously or not, by how they handle (or avoid) biblical passages that are morally challenging or troubling; they will be giving moral lessons by what issues they address or ignore and by what they say about those with whom they disagree on those issues. They will be shaping character by what they say or leave unsaid in the counseling session and by how they respond to the behavior, praiseworthy or otherwise, that is displayed in the communities they lead. Furthermore, they will be continually "speaking with their lives," as the Quakers say, for they will be taken as moral exemplars and role models (whether wisely and fairly or not), which is an aspect of the office that cannot be ignored.

Recognizing that the minister bears special responsibility for the moral formation of youth and adults alike invites reflection about the nature of leadership and care in a congregation, a body that must be a moral community if it is to maintain its identity as the church. The work of formation requires not only explicit teaching and preaching but also fostering relationships that balance patience and humility with the willingness to confront issues honestly. All of these aspects of pastoral ministry call out for the need to address the particular character of moral leadership and for practical tools and guidance. Yet these topics receive very little attention in books in ministerial ethics, which tend to focus on ethics for ministers rather than on ministers as ethicists.[5] I hope to remedy this deficiency.

This first set of reasons leads us to a second set. As leaders in processes of moral reflection and judgment, as well as moral argument and decision, pastors are required to develop a certain set of skills and sensitivities. But because ministers will continually be preaching by behavior and teaching by example, they must also become certain kinds of people: not only people who possess

---

5. Rebekah Miles's *The Pastor as Moral Guide* (Minneapolis: Fortress, 1999) is an exception, but it concentrates on guidance in the context of individual counseling.

certain knowledge and techniques but also people whose character is shaped in particular ways. This necessity is made even more urgent by the difficulty of the role a pastor is called to fill and by the distinctive moral risks and demands that are built into it.

Just how perilous this calling can be is not always acknowledged in the literature. To read some of what is written about the ethics of ministry, one would suppose that the task is merely to explain and justify the applicable rules. That way, ministers will understand why personal and church funds must not be commingled, pastoral duties must not be shirked, professional confidences must not be casually divulged, and congregants must not be used as a way to meet one's own emotional or sexual needs. While these are all sound and laudable principles, I doubt that they are frequently violated because of a failure to understand the rules. Rather, it is because the capacity to recognize and fulfill those obligations when they come under pressure is lost—lost to confusion, to desperation, to isolation and loneliness and self-doubt, all of which obscure vision and dissipate the energy and hope required to sustain moral integrity amid the challenges of life in ministry.

There are, to be sure, wolves among the shepherds, unscrupulous and predatory persons who seek their offices precisely in order to exploit them. But both observation and research suggest that these are very much the exception and not the rule.[6] Most pastors who lose their way do so because they lose themselves, in a sense, and grasp at anything (approval, admiration, celebrity, inflated authority, money, sex, or the unhealthy dependency of those they lead) to fill the void they experience. None of this lessens the destructiveness of violations, and none of it excuses pastoral misconduct. Whether or not pastors feel powerful, they wield enormous power and are responsible for the devastation that can come with its misdirection and abuse. It is altogether appropriate that those who violate the trust they have been given be held accountable. But it is not enough to elaborate the rules of ministerial conduct, as if they in

6. Fortune, *Is Nothing Sacred?*, 47.

themselves could prevent transgressions. It is not enough to create legal and administrative processes for responding to offenses after the fact. While necessary, such responses will always be too little and too late. It is vastly more helpful to understand how those who begin with an intention to serve end up doing harm, to identify the factors that contribute to or reduce that risk, and thus to help prevent misconduct before the harm is done.

To do so, we must probe more deeply into the dynamics that lead to moral confusion and collapse. We must identify the structural features of pastoral ministry that create particular challenges for pastors, challenges that are greater not less for those most personally invested in their ministry. We also need to recognize the distortions of pastoral practice that begin in ways far subtler and more insidious than the sex scandals that attract media attention. We must see these commonplace vices for what they are: early signs of moral and spiritual corrosion that weaken the church and its ministry, even when they lead to no more egregious offenses. I aim to explore what puts ministers as human beings at risk, to help them acknowledge and understand the vulnerabilities that all human beings share, and to help them address these vulnerabilities in safe and appropriate ways. Ultimately, recognizing the profound link between moral performance and spiritual practice will help ministers to develop patterns of life and sustain virtues that will protect them and those they serve.

This book examines all the ways pastors are called upon to be moral theologians in residence for the communities they serve. I first discuss how pastors teach and model Christian ethics (chap. 1). I then offer particular guidance for how this can be done more consciously and constructively in preaching (chap. 2), teaching (chap. 3), and offering pastoral care and counsel (chap. 4). I conclude by discussing the challenges as well as the important opportunities created by the de facto role-model aspect of ministry, perhaps the dimension of ordained life that seminary students reflect on and prepare for least (chap. 5). For those who desire to go more deeply into the topics discussed in the final chapter, I will treat them more fully in a companion volume.[7] There I will focus on the second set of concerns I have identified: the necessity and risks of pastoral power, the spiritual dynamics at work in the minister's role, and strategies for managing those unavoidable risks wisely and faithfully.

7. Sondra Wheeler, *Sustaining Ministry: Foundations and Practices for Serving Faithfully* (Grand Rapids: Baker Academic, forthcoming).

1

The Minister as Ethicist

Ethics between the Lines

Despite the title of this chapter, I realize that the great majority of those who answer a call to Christian ministry have not set out to become ethicists. Most will serve in churches (or hospitals or schools or some other setting) devoted to the praise of God, the proclamation of the kingdom, and the meeting of human needs, not in the academy. So it would not make sense to try to equip all pastors for, say, teaching the history and philosophical foundations of Christian moral thought or explaining Thomas Aquinas's insights regarding the elements of freedom and constraint in human acts. (Although, for what it's worth, this is fascinating and important stuff.) I aim to resist the temptation that besets all academics to try to excite everyone else about the aspects of their disciplines that interest them.

Instead, I want to take seriously the tasks and the needs of those who are called to pastoral ministry or chaplaincy, recognizing that the finer points of moral theory and the more technical aspects of ethics may be of little immediate use to them. Yet the minister is probably the only professional practitioner of Christian ethics most

congregants will ever get to know, a fact that has many implications for the practice of ministry. And if you suppose that such a
description does not apply to you, I would like to make the case
that all who perform the routine tasks of ministry will be doing
moral theology—the exposition of how their theological commitments shape their lives in the world—every day, whether they
think of it that way or not.

To begin with the most obvious, those of you who serve in
churches (and in other ministry settings as well) act as ethicists
in preaching. You convey judgments about what is central and
important in forming and living a Christian life by choosing which
biblical texts to preach on and by choosing what to emphasize
within a given passage. You also teach by default in what texts you
ignore or actively avoid, choosing to offer a topical sermon on the
week in which a particularly challenging passage comes up in the
lectionary. You teach ethics explicitly through what you say about
passages that raise moral issues but also tacitly through what you
assume or leave unsaid—as, for example, when a minister breezes
past the advice in 1 Peter for slaves and women to imitate Christ
by accepting the unjust authority placed over them (2:18–3:6)
without stopping to deal with analogous modern instances of
injustice in police misconduct or domestic abuse. You serve as an
ethicist through what you preach about perennial moral problems
(violence, oppression, infidelity, greed) as well as in the problems
you avoid naming or addressing at all. And whatever moral issues
you choose to address from the pulpit, you teach central lessons
in Christian ethics by how you talk about those who hold other
points of view.

Apart from preaching, ministers in any setting teach in one
form or another. This activity, too, always includes aspects of ethics, whether intended or not. Simple matters, like which church
groups or subjects are deemed worthy of your teaching time, are
full of implications about who and what is most important in the
life of the community. Furthermore, not only the content but also
the method you use in teaching carries lessons in Christian ethics.

What sources do you draw upon in coming to understand a topic, and which have the most weight? How do you reckon with differences between those sources? How do you use the authority of the classroom, and how do you draw out and make use of the ideas and experiences of others? All these practical decisions offer moral lessons in themselves. In the Christian education of adolescents and adults, as in preaching, much is conveyed just through which topics are addressed and which are set aside either as unimportant or as too difficult to handle. If you *do* take on topics that are painful or disputed, then how you approach these areas will be as important as what you say about them. Especially instructive is how you deal with moral disagreement in the society at large, in the church, and within your particular community. How much real ambiguity do you allow for in making moral judgments about complex matters? How tentative or provisional are the positions offered on such issues? In matters of controversy, to what extent do you open the possibility that your view rather than your opponent's might be incorrect? All such attitudes and presuppositions fall under the broad sweep of ethics, which includes habits of heart and mind as well as norms of behavior.

Woven into and underneath all discussions of ethics in the church is an underlying issue of central significance. What is the relationship between Christian faith and moral life? Is Christian life simply a matter of trusting in "the righteousness of God through faith in Jesus Christ" (Rom. 3:22), so that Christian ethics begins and ends with throwing oneself at the foot of the cross? Or conversely, does it all depend on one's behavior, so that (as the letter of James suggests) true religion is "to care for widows and orphans in their distress" (1:27)? Does that mean we need not worry too much about what—or whether—we believe? Or is the relationship between faith and morality more complicated than either of these texts taken alone can indicate? Some answers to these questions, however unformed, are implied by the patterns and practices of a community. How and to what extent are ethical questions taken up in the proclamation and instruction of a given congregation?

How are these matters related to its core theological commitments? The day-to-day life of a Christian organization embodies an ethical viewpoint and a sort of unspoken moral theology. By the nature of the enterprise, all Christian teachers, and thus all ministers, are also teachers of ethics.

While preaching and teaching Sunday school are clearly activities peculiar to religious communities, the giving of care and counsel may seem like one of the services that ministers provide in common with many other professionals. Psychiatrists, psychologists, clinical social workers, marriage therapists, and even the emerging specialty of "life coaches"—all are among those who offer support, advice, and therapeutic assistance to individuals, couples, and families in a variety of situations. These professionals are trained in a variety of disciplines and possess a range of skills. They represent diverse methods, approaches, and schools of thought, as indeed clergy may bring different levels of training and experience and different tools, resources, and theoretical frameworks to their work in pastoral care and counseling. What makes ministers and pastoral counselors distinct as a group from other caregivers is that they are grounded in part in some religious tradition and receive part of their authority from that tradition.

This foundation means that pastoral counselors are not neutral in their work but represent a particular, theologically informed view of the world and of the human being. They do not begin their encounters with people seeking help from a position of agnosticism about what is true and important, and they cannot adopt a posture of indifference to these commitments or their implications when counselees step into the pastor's study. Judgments about good and evil, conduct that is worthy of praise or blame, and paths that lead to human flourishing or impoverishment all depend on what is real and true about human beings and the world they inhabit. For this reason, the counseling activities of ministers always have ethical aspects to them. A minister cannot simply accept uncritically whatever life goal or strategy parishioners offer and neutrally set about helping them to achieve the proffered aims by whatever means come to hand. Rather, the minister must engage with the counselee in the work of discernment, of coming to moral clarity and judgment, and must call the person to faithfulness in this work as an aspect of discipleship.

Let me hasten to acknowledge that the Christian faith is not uniform. There are significant differences in theological interpretation and resultant moral judgments among the various Christian traditions and indeed within them. Nor is it even the case that two people who subscribe to the identical statement of faith will always come to the same ethical judgment in a particular case. The point here is merely that in a community of faith, life choices and decisions are recognized as *moral* decisions; they are aspects of living out one's faith and not merely matters of personal taste or preference. They are, therefore, fit matters for discussion, subject to ethical evaluation and critique, possibly calling for affirmation or even for reproach. This is true whether the congregant (or even the pastor!) wishes to deal with morality directly or not.

Sometimes, of course, congregants come explicitly seeking moral counsel. Other times they may come seeking permission to follow a course of action that has obvious ethical problems. Occasionally they come having already decided upon such a course and want help in carrying it out. ("Please help me tell my wife that I am leaving her for my girlfriend so she doesn't get too upset"—an actual example!) And then there are the times people do not come, but you and those around them desperately wish they would. If you are a pastor—a word that, after all, means "shepherd"—what do you do when a parishioner proposes or undertakes some patently outrageous course of conduct? Or conversely, when someone in your care grieves and agonizes over some moral decision that cannot be made any more faithfully than it already has been? At least some of the time, to be a pastor is to offer more than what we commonly call "moral support": it is, with all humility and some trembling, to offer moral guidance.

The final category of what I have called "ethics between the lines" in ministry is the subtlest and in many ways the most challenging of all. It comes of the fact that, whether you like it or not, fairly or unfairly, as a minister you are taken as a model—an exemplar of a faithful Christian life. There is a potent opportunity as well as a serious responsibility in this: many have been inspired to greater practical faithfulness by the Quaker saying, "Let your life speak." But of course, in a broader sense your life *is* speaking all the time, especially if you are the visible leader of a community. The question is, what is it saying? And because communication always depends on both members in the exchange, what your behavior is taken to say will never be fully in your control, nor will your actions always be interpreted generously or even reasonably.

If as a pastor you are seen doing something, others may twist this as permission to serve their own agenda, even if the circumstances are not really comparable. ("Even the minister drinks. Get off my back about a couple of shots on the way home from work! I'm fine to drive!") If you have had a bad day and a splitting headache, and you snap at a parishioner who is being domineering in a meeting, it is not just your conduct in that moment that will be subject to criticism. Your leadership and even your calling may be questioned. More broadly still, moral failures that become known are taken not only to reflect badly upon ministers but also to cast doubt on the faith they represent, as we have seen in the public scandals over sex and money that have plagued the church over the past few decades. Finally, and deepest of all, beyond the requirement of modeling faithful discipleship day to day, there are some occasions—at the Communion Table or beside a penitent or at the bedside of the dying—where the minister's role is nothing less than to embody the presence of Christ. It is not obvious how those who serve in ministry can take the weight of this role seriously without self-deception or collapse.

By now I hope I have made clear why ministers cannot avoid doing ethics as part of their ordinary work. As a pastor, you function as an ethicist in a variety of ways, and in some way in almost every activity you undertake, if only as an example whose conduct will be taken as a standard by members of your congregation. If you serve in another kind of institution, in a school or in a hospital, in the military or as a chaplain for police and firefighters, the particular shape of your ministry may change, but it will still include the elements of proclamation and instruction, giving counsel and modeling discipleship. Whether or not this was part of your plan, having entered into ministry, you are the moral theologian in residence for the community you serve.

The Church as a Moral Community

Every human being of ordinary mental capacity over the age of seven or eight is "doing ethics," at least in the basic sense of making choices that have moral dimensions. Similarly, all Christians can be said to be "doing moral theology" in that they are living out some version of a Christian life, whether they are reflecting on it or not. But ministers are a special instance of this general truth because they have undertaken to lead a congregation or some other Christian community. Such a role draws upon all three dimensions of moral existence: what one understands, what one does, and who one is. It includes the formal leadership of worship and instruction and the administration of the church as an organization. It also includes the informal aspects of personal presence and example, the building of relationships, and the modeling of a shared life. Formal and informal aspects of ministry are intertwined, and both are vital to effectiveness. Leadership involves a delicate dance of speaking and listening, influencing others and being influenced by them, and developing the common ethos that makes an organization healthy and effective. This is true even in secular organizations, the government, or for-profit enterprises, whose leaders must forge a common purpose and a shared commitment to it in order to accomplish their goals. But a church is a distinct case in that a church must be a moral community in the deepest sense in order to retain its identity as a witness to the gospel and a sign of the reign of God.

To be a moral community in this comprehensive sense is first of all to be grounded as a place of theological reflection. It is to be rooted in study, thought, and prayer about the practical implications of Christianity's central claim: that God has acted in the life, death, and resurrection of Jesus of Nazareth to redeem and reclaim the world as God's own. Most Christian traditions send their prospective pastors for extensive education to equip them to lead such reflection, training them in tools of biblical analysis and the history and structure of Christian thought. But the role of a minister is not properly to study and reflect *for* the community in the sense of doing it on their behalf. Rather, it is to invite all members of the community into the shared work of reflection, a dimension of loving God with one's whole mind that is part of the first and greatest commandment (Mark 12:30 and parallels). Christians are those gripped by an extraordinary story: how God in Jesus has followed us even into flesh to break the cycle of sin and death that holds us and the whole creation captive. How does this astonishing act grasp our lives and open us to new possibilities? What does a life set free from fear and futility look like? If the whole of Christian existence can be summed up as loving God and our neighbors, how do we discern together the concrete shape of love in our own time and place? These are not questions only for the ordained but for all who are members of the body of Christ in the world.

From this foundation the other aspects of life as a moral community arise. The people nurtured into Christian faith are also gathered in prayerful attention concerning the particular gifts and calling of this community of faith and of the individuals who compose it. This Spirit-guided work of learning to see the world as God intends it, and to recognize one's place in bringing that world to light, is what the tradition calls moral discernment. Together in worship and prayer, in the study of Scripture and the study of the world they are called to serve, with the help of the Holy Spirit, Christians seek to know their vocation and respond to God's call. But the path of faithfulness is often challenging.

The ongoing communal task of growing into people who have the skills and the character to fulfill their vocation is the long work of moral formation, and it has countless dimensions. We are shaped by all we see and hear—by the stories we treasure and the examples we lift up, by the lives of the saints and the steady disciplines of prayer and worship, where we learn to give up our illusions of control and remember with gratitude that God reigns. And we are formed by the company we keep: the friendships we nurture and the unlikely companions God gives us for the journey, the people God bestows on us who support or challenge, comfort or irritate us, the concrete and particular neighbors we are given to love and to learn from.

The deep, subtle shaping of how we see ourselves and the world, of what we hope for and imagine, what we love and trust and fear—all of this is part of sustained participation in a community of faith. This formation of character bears its most visible fruit in the mission and ministry of the congregation, but it also shows itself in the internal conversation that guides and propels that ministry, the conversation about the shape of a faithful life and the demands of discipleship. Such conversation is essential to the ongoing health and vitality of the congregation, for without it even once-vibrant missional programs tend to become matters of rote, based on "we've always done in that way" and not on the present gifts of the church or the actual needs of the wider community it serves. And apart from the constant renewal of vision and the continuing incorporation of new members with their ideas, gifts, and challenges, churches do not survive the changes that time brings within and outside their walls. Part of seeking a renewed vision and call is grappling with the issues of the day that confront us and trying to find a way forward that is faithful, bearing witness to the good news of God's love and the truth of God's reign over a broken and self-destructive human world.

This means that to be itself, the church must be a place of continuing moral conversation, a community where it is safe to struggle with confusion and disagreement, because what unites us is stronger than what might divide. The truth is that our unity is not a choice but a fact: it is the result of what God has freely done for all of us in common, and it knits us together whether we like it or not. We are sisters and brothers, kin by divine fiat, and we can no more exclude and ignore those we are sure are wrong (as they likely are equally sure about us!) than we can stop inviting Uncle Al to family weddings just because we find him so disagreeable. But we also cannot avoid unpleasantness by dodging real conversations, keeping things on a polite and superficial level where we do not offend but also do not truly engage one another. We need to talk with one another about what is true and important in how we live our daily lives: what is at stake in the promises we keep or break, in the way we earn our money and how we use it, and what it might mean to be a Christian and a citizen. In these and a hundred other arenas, we are giving testimony about what we actually believe and love, hope for or fear, and we need to probe together how that testimony conforms to what we say in church on Sunday morning. To abandon that aspect of the church's common life is to settle for being something less than the church, a place of comfort without accountability, of service to the members rather than service to God, who calls the church into being as a living light to the world.

To sustain such a conversation is not easy, and it is not for the fainthearted, for it involves not just observation and discussion of issues in the abstract but also encouragement in the challenging discipline of learning to conform the witness of our lives to the witness of the gospel. It means learning to listen as well as to speak, to suspend certainty on matters about which we hold firm and passionate convictions so that we may be open to learning from others. And when that learning leads to the realization that we or someone else has turned aside from the path of faithfulness, then the community becomes the place of reform and reconciliation, where the wanderer is invited to repentance, forgiveness, and restoration. If this sounds uncomfortable, time consuming, and socially awkward, it frequently is. It is also deeply counter to our culture, which tends to treat all morality as a matter of personal taste and entirely private judgment. But for those who dare take it, this path of shared moral discernment and discipline is rich and life giving, an indispensable means of growing together in holiness, into the very likeness of Christ in the world.

However, if the church's work of becoming a moral community helps us to avoid the risks of uncritical accommodation to whatever values prevail in a given society, it is not without risks of its own. On one side is the perennial temptation to focus on the failings and offenses of other people rather than on our own and to confuse the necessity of truthful speech with the sins of self-righteousness and condemnation. Most of us who have spent years in the church have seen instances of these deformations. On the other side is the danger of continual anxious self-examination and constant fear of offending God. This is the failing that Christian tradition calls "scrupulosity" and warns against for its ability to undermine joy and trust in the gracious mercy of God. This is perhaps less common in generations shaped by the therapeutic maxim "I'm OK—You're OK," but it still rears its head in the church, as most experienced pastors can attest. It is no small feat to form and sustain healthy life in such a community, even guided and nourished by the Holy Spirit.

By now it should be clear why the church, which must be a moral community to be fully itself, calls for a distinctive kind of leadership. It is not enough to administer the organization efficiently, not enough to display exegetical and rhetorical skill in preaching, not enough even to be a caring presence in trouble—though all of this is needed. To be able to foster a conversation at once intimate and broad about the shape of faithfulness requires all of a leader's gifts: knowledge and interpersonal skills, spiritual maturity, and all the cultivated patience and humility required of anyone who seeks to lead a community toward a character not yet fully realized in oneself. While much of the capacity for this work depends on the deeper elements of emotional health and spiritual nourishment,[1] I

---

1. I treat these elements in my companion volume, *Sustaining Ministry*.

want to begin in the arena of knowledge, by providing a few basic tools as resources for the minister who undertakes to nurture a Christian community through intentional moral discernment and formation. These tools will be of service to us as we examine the ethical dimensions of the pastor's work as preacher, teacher, and giver of moral counsel. They will also be helpful when we return to speak of the challenges of being a moral example in the church.

What Good Is a Theory?

I have already acknowledged that not all the aspects of Christian ethics that are of interest to the academic specialist are of immediate use to those called to ministry. A vast technical literature analyzes human acts and judgments, explores the nature and limits of moral freedom, and examines the inner dynamics of motivation and self-awareness. Alongside different accounts of human beings, this literature offers widely varying accounts of the relation between Christian faith and moral life and competing views of whether (and if so, how) we can know and do what is good. These broad treatments are joined by reams of material about particular issues and areas of concern—political ethics, economic ethics, medical ethics, and so on—if not quite ad infinitum, then certainly too many for even the specialist to pursue them all.

But this does not mean that none of the resources of ethics as an academic field are helpful to those who are charged with leading churches or other Christian organizations. I would argue that there are few things of greater practical value than a good theory, for a theory is just an abstract and general account of what something is and how it works. What makes it useful is that it can be applied to any number of cases in a way that illuminates and clarifies both what they have in common and what makes them distinct. Accordingly, at its most fundamental level a moral theory is an explanation of the meaning of moral language—that is, what we are saying when we use ordinary terms like "right" or "wrong" and "good" or "evil." Embedded in any such explanation is an idea about how we come to moral judgments (or perhaps how we ought to come to them!) and how such judgments can be explained and defended when doubts or disagreements arise. Also implicit in any fully developed moral theory is a picture of moral life, of what we are doing when we "do ethics," and of what sort of creatures we must be to do it well.

I want to offer a short survey of how disciplined reflection about moral life has been shaped in Western thought, what such reflection is good for, and how to help others engage in it. For some readers this will be a review of material covered in a long-ago course in college or seminary, while for others it will be new. Whichever group you fall into, this summary is brief and nontechnical enough not to be burdensome while showing how it might provide a framework for leading moral conversation in the church. The aim in this is not to fix the shape of the community's conversation, much less to determine the conclusions that might be reached in it. It is rather to deepen and enrich that conversation and to help it achieve, if not consensus, at least mutual understanding and sympathy. For that purpose, I will introduce the three broad families of moral theory, name some of their strengths and weaknesses, and say a little bit about the theological foundations on which they have drawn in Christian usage.

In the course of this survey, I will highlight the connections between moral theory (how we understand moral language) and moral method (how we come to a decision). I will also discuss the connection between the theoretical perspective we adopt and how we see the world: what appears to us as a moral issue to begin with and what seems most imporant about it. Most centrally for our purposes, I aim to show how familiarity with the various languages of ethics can help us to broaden what we pay attention to and the questions we learn to ask.

The Ethics of Duty

Of the families of ethical theory, the ethics of duty is often the most familiar, the taken-for-granted form in which people first encounter morality as a category. Put most simply, *the ethics of duty evaluates acts in terms of whether they fulfill or violate one's obligations.* These obligations may be expressed in various ways, as rules or laws or principles, and they may be quite particular ("You shall not charge interest on loans to another Israelite" [Deut. 23:19]) or altogether general ("You shall love your neighbor as yourself" [Lev. 19:18; Mark 12:31 and parallels]) Obligations may also be grounded in varying kinds of authority: taken as the commands of God, like the Scripture quoted above, or as the laws binding a particular society ("Congress shall make no law respecting the establishment of religion").[2] They may be something one has voluntarily taken on, like the duties one assumes by taking an oath of office, or they may be implicit in the situation one is born into, as having received care and benefits from one's parents creates a duty of gratitude. Or duties may be in a certain sense owed to oneself, as a form of respect for the sort of being one is. For example, accounts of humans as rational creatures ground a whole branch of ethical thought wherein a person is obliged to act in accord with reason.[3] In this way, obligations of equity and consistency and fair reciprocity, along with respect for others and honesty, are understood to be founded in the nature of human beings as rational moral actors. To act contrary to such duties is to act unreasonably, and thus less humanly, betraying one's true nature and forfeiting its freedom.

These are only the broad strokes on a very large and detailed canvas, but they are enough to suggest what is helpful and clarifying in approaches to ethics grounded in obligation. They help us to step back from ourselves, from our desires and feelings, and from self-interest so that we can see the situation with a wider lens and a greater degree of objectivity. We may have an impulsive desire to take what is not rightfully ours, but we recognize the legitimacy

2. US Constitution, Amendment I.
3. This description could be applied to all forms of ethics based on "rational universalizability," such as all of those derived from the work of Immanuel Kant. It could also describe many forms of natural law ethics from Aristotle to Thomas Aquinas.

of the rule against stealing. We may in furious anger want to hurt someone, but both moral and legal obligations restrain us. A situation may arise where it would be easier and more convenient to lie to a friend than to deal with the truth. But it is not long before we ask ourselves, "Doesn't this person deserve the truth?" or "How would I feel if this person I trust lied to me?" The language of duty presses us back from what we *want* to do in the moment to what we *ought* to do, from the act that might be satisfying or beneficial to us as individuals to the act that we can justify as right and good and fair in our relationships with others. Clear rules and principles can be of great help in circumstances where we are either confused or tempted, serving as lines we know we should not cross.

However, true though it may be, this description leaves some things out of the account. For one thing, it does not address the fact that the application of principles and rules is not always simple or straightforward. Most of us would argue that there are limits to property rights, for instance, times when dire need might overcome a person's claim on what belongs to him or her. Thus Thomas Aquinas argues that a starving man who takes bread from the surplus of another as a last resort does not break the commandment against stealing.[4] Even more confusing, duties may conflict with one another. What are we to do when a promise to keep someone's secret runs up against the obligation to tell the truth when we are asked a direct question? Or more simply, when the obligation to care for one person is at war with the duty to care for another? There are strategies both formal and informal for thinking through and resolving such conflicts, and I do not want to suggest that just because rules are not absolute or self-interpreting they can offer us no guidance. It is often said that hard cases make bad law; they make bad ethics too. The point here is merely that rules and principles *require* interpretation and application if they are to offer practical help, and much depends on the wisdom and insight with which that work is done.

4. *Summa Theologica* I-II.66.7.

It is also important to note that the ethics of duty (like any system of moral thought) has characteristic weaknesses as well as characteristic strengths. One of those weaknesses is a relative lack of adaptability. Principles, being more general, typically have some degree of flexibility built in, but rules that work well in one context may require modification or complete rethinking if they are to serve the good they were meant to in another. Duty ethics (again, like any moral paradigm) also has characteristic forms of corruption and decline. This is seen when principles or rules that express our obligations are made utterly fixed and unyielding and treated as if they could offer a completeness and certainty that removes the need to pay attention to anything beyond the formal requirement of the law. If the great benefit of the ethics of obligation is clarity and the pressure toward objectivity, its corresponding risk is rigidity and narrowness of vision. It is possible for the reason and purpose of the law to be obscured and its function of guarding the integrity of the community lost, leaving only the letter that kills and not the Spirit that gives life (cf. 2 Cor. 3:6).

Despite these issues, the strong theological foundations for this way of approaching ethics are obvious to anyone with even a casual acquaintance with the Bible. There God is met as the Creator who speaks the universe into being, whose Word is law in the most profound sense of bringing what it declares into existence. With the advent of humankind, God is shown as lawgiver in the more ordinary sense. In the narrative of Genesis 3, God offers the bounty of the garden to the human couple with one prohibition: the fruit of the tree of the knowledge of good and evil. After human transgression breaks the first peace of creation, the relationship between God and humanity is repaired through a series of covenants in which mutual obligations are framed by laws and promises binding God and the people. From a Christian standpoint, these covenants reach their final fulfillment with the coming of Jesus Christ, who declares a new covenant sealed in his own blood. But even here it is possible to speak of the "law of Christ," fulfilled by obedience to the double commandment to love

God with a whole heart and to love the neighbor as oneself. The language of law and obligation serves to honor the sovereignty of God and to highlight the seriousness of the requirement that humans respond to God's claim.

The Ethics of Consequences

If the ethics of obligation is the first form of ethical thought most people recognize, the ethics of consequences may be the form they most readily resort to in making daily decisions. This is true both in the arena of personal choices and in matters of public policy, particularly when some conflict arises between competing goals or desires. One common application of this moral theory is encountered in the risk-benefit analysis that guides decisions in human enterprises from medicine to transportation policy to tax law. At its most basic, *consequentialist ethics understands the meaning of right action to be action that brings about the best results for all those affected by it.* Acts that are likely to bring about poor results for those affected by them (whether actually adverse or merely less good than available alternatives) are judged morally wrong. By these calculations, unpredictable accidents (like a fatal car crash on the way to take a neighbor to the doctor), however dire, are not part of the moral judgment upon the act unless one has somehow contributed to them. The results by which acts are to be evaluated are only those that can reasonably be foreseen.

While this broad definition holds true across the family of consequentialist forms of ethics, there is as much scope and variety in this branch of ethical theory as we saw in the ethics of obligation. To begin with, the underlying rationale for the pursuit of the best results can be grounded in different ways. It can be rooted in the love of neighbor when that is understood as beneficence, doing good or offering benefit to others. It can also be founded in the nature of distinctively human acts, acts that are chosen and deliberate rather than done by instinct or reflex. To be human is to act "on purpose," as we say, to set out to bring about a foreseen result that is more desirable than alternatives. And just as the ethics of duty can be grounded in the human capacity for reason, so can the ethics of consequences: on this view, it is simply irrational to act in a way that does not produce the best possible result, a repudiation of our nature and capacities.

There are also multiple accounts of the nature of the goods and harms that should direct our choices. People who hold to consequentialist ethics argue about how these goods and harms should be identified and defined, whether all goods are instances of a single thing, like pleasure or utility, or whether there are diverse goods. They also dispute whether goods and harms are the same for everyone or depend on individual preferences. Finally, consequentialist theorists disagree as to whether decisions should be based on the consequences of each individual act (e.g., Will the truth or a lie bring about the best result in this particular case?) or on the pattern of action that is most beneficial overall (e.g., Will it be better for everyone if people can have reasonable confidence in the truthfulness of others' statements?).

Some of the strengths of this form of moral reasoning and judgment are evident. Consequentialist ethics is highly flexible and enables one to take account of special circumstances as well as changes in historical context. It accords with at least some of our commonsense moral intuitions about wanting to have things come out for the best. Also, the moral vision this form of ethics holds out is notable for being inclusive and egalitarian. Common to all forms of consequentialism is the insistence that all the effects of our actions count, no matter whom they might fall upon. Moreover, in the balancing of good and bad effects that is part of the calculation of best result, the effects on all parties count equally: effects on self or others, on friends or enemies, on those of any social status. It is no coincidence that utilitarian moral thinkers (the earliest advocates of consequentialist ethics) were among the first to argue for the equal rights of women and for laws to protect laborers. Those who simply do whatever brings about the best result for themselves without regard for others are not acting as utilitarians; by the light of this theory, they are merely behaving immorally. A disciplined attention to consequences will teach us to look at long-term as well as short-term results and to accept responsibility for all that can reasonably be foreseen to result from our decisions.

As is often the case, the weaknesses of consequentialism as a moral framework have the same roots as its strengths. The flexibility that allows one to take account of circumstances can also make room for rationalization and special pleading when one's own interests figure into the judgment of results. The even-handed objectivity required for a fair weighing of better and worse consequences is hard to come by and hard to sustain. Even more basic, it is not clear how we are to do the moral calculus required in weighing out the mix of good and bad effects of actions when those effects are of different kinds and affect different people. Does a small benefit to fifty people outweigh a significant harm to one? And where is the scale on which we can weigh very different kinds of goods (the overall benefit of funding an art museum against that of improving vaccination rates, for instance)? Finally, judging the morality of actions based on the results for all of those affected requires a high degree of confidence in our ability to foresee and quantify all the results that flow from those actions. However, anyone who has studied history or public policy knows that it is in large part a story of unintended consequences and unforeseen effects.

Still, the basic insight that human beings act for reasons and aim at some result holds true. Moreover, the capacity to order our actions so as to achieve some end is a fundamental aspect of being rational and morally responsible creatures, a part of how we are made in the image of God. And no account of moral life that ignores the actual consequences of our decisions for us and for others can claim to be fully Christian. The witness of Scripture, with its detailed instructions about practical matters from family life to commercial exchanges to the treatment of farm animals, makes it clear that material life and well-being matter. Likewise, the life and flourishing of nonhuman creatures is important if only because God has made and blessed them and entrusted them to human care. The ethics of the apostle Paul may be centered upon what he calls "the obedience of faith" (Rom. 1:5) and the law of love (Rom. 13:8), but he can still summarize the shape of Christian obligation succinctly: "So then, as we have opportunity, let us do good to all persons, especially to those who are of the household of faith" (Gal. 6:10 RSV, alt.).

The Ethics of Virtue

Whereas both the ethics of duty and the ethics of consequences focus upon guiding or evaluating particular acts and decisions, the ethics of virtue or character takes a broader view. It is interested in what we do as, first of all, an expression of and a contribution to who we are: what kind of persons we are revealing ourselves to be and what kind we are becoming as we act and decide. Rather than evaluating each act as meeting or failing to meet an obligation, virtue ethics asks what is involved in becoming a trustworthy and reliable person, one who has the capacity to recognize and fulfill one's duties. Instead of calculating how each act contributes to a goal in the world outside of us, character ethics focuses on their contributions to the goal within us: the goal of becoming a morally excellent person. Accordingly, *the ethics of character understands the meaning of right action to be the action that would be taken by a person who possessed the required virtues*, who would be able to judge and to enact what goodness looks like in the particular situation. In this way, character ethics has aspects of the other families of ethical theories, incorporating stable moral principles (such as the cardinal virtue of justice) and attention to the concrete circumstances in which judgments must be made.

This way of thinking about moral life as fundamentally a matter of character is reflected in the way we commonly talk about people, whether actual individuals we know or the "characters" of history and fiction. We offer moral descriptions of people not by listing their individual acts but by naming the reliable patterns they show over time, patterns we regard as expressions of who they are. Of course, the traits we identify are not perfectly uniform and unchanging. A person who is generally patient may lose her temper occasionally, and we all know (to our sorrow) that even good people can fail dramatically or gradually be compromised and corrupted. However, most of us also have the happy experience of seeing persons develop with time and nurture positive traits that they lacked in the past. (Otherwise, hope of moral reform and spiritual transformation in the church would be hard to sustain.) Despite these cautions, in general we experience our own lives and the lives of those whom we know not as a series of disconnected situations and decisions but as narratives. They take the form of stories in which we and others become relatively steady and coherent personalities, including moral personalities, with reliable traits of character. Our ordinary moral conversation bears witness to this experience.

The ethics of virtue is not, however, altogether uninterested in particular moral judgments or acts: one definition of virtue is the capacity to act rightly when it is difficult. But virtue ethics tends to see right action as dependent upon things that are prior to and deeper than any single decision. These are the dispositions, habits, and skills cultivated over a lifetime that enable us to see a situation accurately and judge wisely the right thing to do. They also equip us reliably to act upon the correct judgment when it is reached, something that is frequently hard to do even when the judgment itself is quite clear. These cultivated habits and skills are what we call the virtues.

Here as in the other families of moral theory there is both variation and historical development over time. But the ethics of virtue as it has shaped Christian thought in the West is to a large extent descended from the work of thirteenth-century scholar and mystic Thomas Aquinas. He set out to integrate classical philosophy (particularly Aristotle's) with Scripture and the medieval Catholic tradition, incorporating the moral thought of the ancient Greeks into a theological structure grounded in God's work as Creator,

Redeemer, and Sustainer. The result for Christian ethics was an account that retained the four cardinal virtues of prudence, justice, fortitude, and temperance, understanding them to be the fruit of nature as it is developed in a good community. These were the virtues that equipped human beings to build and inhabit a good society. To these Thomas added the three theological virtues of faith, hope, and love, familiar from 1 Corinthians 13. These were understood as supernatural, the gifts of divine grace, which fit us for communion with God and the saints. The theological virtues also reach back and transform the natural virtues so that each virtue takes on a new character as grace reorders them toward our ultimate destiny in God. The development and refinement of these capacities for goodness is the lifelong work of every human being. They form the heart of moral life and offer the fulfillment of our potential as beings created in the image of God.

The strengths of virtue approaches to moral understanding should be easy to recognize. Their focus on who we are rather than on what we decide in a given moment corresponds to our sense of ourselves as moral beings. We are characters who develop and grow over time into a measure of stability, who face setbacks and surprises, but whose reality cannot fully be conveyed in a list of decision points. Virtue ethics teaches us to pay attention to who we are becoming, to how we are being formed or deformed by the characters we admire, the models we imitate, and the practices we adopt. It draws our attention to the most enduring product of our moral existence, which is neither the codes we adopt nor the good we accomplish, but rather the selves we become in the process.

The ethics of character also has obvious connections to one of the prevalent languages of the New Testament. There, the call to holiness is expressed not in terms of obligations to fulfill or practical goods to bring about but centrally as being conformed to the likeness of Christ (Rom. 8:29), "transformed by the renewing of [our] minds" so that we "may discern what is . . . good and acceptable and perfect" (Rom. 12:2). Thus Paul speaks of the transformation to be wrought in us by God's grace not in terms of law but of virtues, the "love, joy, peace, patience, kindness, generosity, faithfulness, gentleness, and self-control" that are the fruit of the Holy Spirit (Gal. 5:22–23).

The easy connection between the ethics of virtue and the moral language of the New Testament points toward a limitation as well as a strength. Virtue ethics understands moral life as a kind of inward progress toward a goal, where the virtues are developed skills and habits that enable us to reach this goal. This understanding works well enough in the Christian context, where the ultimate purpose or goal of human existence is broadly agreed upon: to "glorify God and enjoy God forever," to borrow the words of an old catechism. But it is harder to see how we can achieve any degree of consensus about virtue in a social setting where there is very little agreement about what human life is *for*, whether it even has a purpose, or what makes it meaningful or successful. In such a setting, it is easy enough for one to praise as hard-headedness what another would call hard-heartedness, or for one to condemn as weakness what another would call compassion. More than statements of obligation or calculations of benefit and harm, understandings of human excellence and fulfillment depend upon a community and a vision of the human good. In their absence, virtues and vices will seem no more than subjective terms of approval or disapproval, with no claim to truthfulness or authority.

This brings us to a related criticism, that the language of virtue has a kind of frustrating circularity. If right action is defined as the action that would be taken by a person of virtue, and virtues are the capacities that enable us to judge and to act rightly, where and how do we learn to recognize what right action looks like? The answer of classical thought seems to have been that we have to be formed and taught in a good community, one inhabited by persons of virtue. But this just continues the circle, for where are these virtuous persons to come from? Without delving into the various and ingenious answers offered in antiquity, I will merely note that Christians at least have an answer to the problem of what can serve as the model and source of moral goodness. Jesus himself is the model of virtue, and the Holy Spirit is the one by whom we are formed into his likeness.

Ethical Theory and Moral Leadership

Often when I begin teaching a seminary course in ethics, I start by saying what we will *not* accomplish in our fourteen weeks together. Among other things, I say that I will not be able to show students a method for getting the right answer to every ethical question every time, and that I do not expect that we as a group will reach unanimous conclusions about every issue. For some students this is a disappointment, because they are hoping for an end to confusion. For others it is a relief, since they are afraid of being told what to think about complicated and controversial topics. But the fact that ethics as a discipline may not yield certainty on every question or universal agreement on every issue does not mean that it has nothing to offer those who are looking for actual guidance or help in finding the truth. As I hope the preceding survey has shown, what ethics is really good at is probing what we mean to say by calling something right or wrong, good or evil. This in turn helps us to understand some of the disagreements that arise among people who use the same words but mean rather different things by them. Familiarity with moral theory will not lead to the resolution of all conflicts, but it may lead to greater understanding and sympathy for those with whom we disagree. This is vital for the church to be a community of moral conversation and moral discernment.

It may also help us to understand conflicts we feel within ourselves when powerful moral intuitions pull us in different ways. For instance, when the devastation and brutality of war are brought home to us, we think, "Surely this could not be loving our neighbors!" At the same time, we are at a loss for how better to halt the spread of vicious regimes or the madness of genocide, which destroy others who are also our neighbors. This experience of being torn between principles we believe in and consequences we cannot bear is nearly universal. The fact is, none of the three broad approaches to ethics is altogether complete and freestanding, and no normal human being operates with utter disregard for any of them.

The links between different ways of thinking about ethics are built in at the theoretical levels as well as in human experience. We have already seen the close connection between virtues and the capacity for right moral decision and action, understood in light of principles like justice and impartiality. Right doing may be the fruit of right being according to virtue theory, but right action is itself part of what forms character. Thus some notion of what it is right or wrong to do informs the pursuit of virtue. Similarly, no one who is concerned about fulfilling a duty can be indifferent to the effects of actions upon others; for one thing, some of those duties (like gratitude or reciprocity) are framed in terms of offering benefit to someone. Conversely, generally recognized duties like truthfulness and avoiding harm to the innocent continue to make themselves felt even when a careful calculation of overall consequences leads someone to decide that the morally best course requires lying or harming some in order to help others. People in these circumstances continue to experience the tug of the obligation they have overridden for the sake of the best result, even when they remain convinced they have done the right thing.

But beyond analyzing conflicts and understanding disagreements, the most important benefit of familiarity with moral theory for the minister entrusted with moral leadership in a community is that it teaches us to pay attention to all aspects of a moral situation. Each of the three families of ethics highlights a particular dimension of moral life, and each offers particular insights. Each approach leads the inquirer to ask a different set of questions and to become aware of a different set of challenges. Taken together and thoughtfully applied, they can help the pastor to see more keenly all the elements of a complex ethical issue and to lead others into a richer and more complete understanding in turn. Some acquaintance with ethics helps us to ask more and better questions, questions that invite congregants to see a complicated reality in 360 degrees and to enter more deeply into the hard work of moral discernment.

2

Preaching
on Morally Difficult Texts
and Occasions

Why Preaching about Ethics Is Dangerous

Perhaps it did not fully come home to you until after seminary was done—after you had undergone the psychological testing, submitted the endless paperwork, endured your judicatory interview, and passed your ordination exams (or gotten over whatever particular hurdles your own community lovingly placed before you). Even after the ceremonies are over, the Bible and stole bestowed, and all the marks of official responsibility for church leadership are in hand, it may take a while for this obvious fact to sink in: worship happens every seven days (at least), in season and out of it, on good days and bad. And every time it does (or perhaps every other time, if you are lucky enough to share this responsibility), you are expected to preach.

Preaching is the most visible, the most public, the most unavoidable aspect of pastoral ministry, and it is often a significant part of ministry in other contexts as well. It is also the only aspect of a pastor's work that some congregants are exposed to since in most churches there are a substantial number of members who rarely attend any event other than Sunday morning worship. This means that preaching is not only a command performance for you as a pastor but also your single opportunity to instruct, engage, inspire—or at least awaken!—some of the people for whose spiritual nurture you are responsible. This is the reason seminary faculty spend so much time working to hone students' skills at interpreting Scripture in a way that is faithful to the text but also connected to the lives of those for whom they will interpret the Word. It is also why such effort is put into developing students' ability to write and deliver that interpretation in a form that is accessible and interesting without glossing over the depths of the biblical witness or the challenges it presents to our lives.

But the work of the preacher is not limited to applying the techniques of exegesis learned in Bible courses or practicing the skills in rhetoric and public speaking instilled in homiletics class. It is not enough to interpret and present the biblical text. Along with interpreting the passage, the preacher must interpret the community to whom the Word is spoken and the world in which that community is embedded. Is the sanctuary filled with people battered by a hostile world, who come to church for a respite and a source of renewed energy and hope? Is it an aging congregation facing both personal and collective decline and the half-acknowledged prospect of death? Is this an assemblage of hard-striving achievers, perhaps just now coming to suspect how empty such a life can feel, even when all the hurdles are behind them? Whatever the community and the realities it faces, these circumstances must be studied and understood and addressed by the preacher alongside the Scriptures. And the preacher must keep on doing it, week in and week out, across a dramatically diverse array of texts and often for an increasingly transient congregation in a world in which the pace of change continues to accelerate. It is an altogether daunting responsibility. So it is in no way surprising that many preachers—most of them, perhaps—do not readily add to the challenges they face by tackling difficult, morally sensitive, or controversial topics from the pulpit, even when the lectionary texts for the week present them more or less directly.

This reluctance to take on the "hard sayings" of Jesus, the most demanding or perplexing teachings of the apostles, or the passages that touch upon issues that have become the subject of painful controversy and division within the church is understandable. Beyond that, exercising some restraint is often wise. Diving into the most profound of spiritual depths ("Present your bodies as a living sacrifice" [Rom. 12:1]) or the most stunning of practical demands ("None of you can become my disciple if you do not give up all your possessions" [Luke 14:33]) is no way to begin the conversation. Neither is it helpful to start with the summary judgment "Whoever divorces his wife and marries another commits adultery" (Mark 10:11), an absolute prohibition somehow less often noted than those concerning same-sex relations. These texts are there; they are not safely tucked away in obscure passages in Numbers but are squarely located in the New Testament and many are placed in Jesus's own mouth. But dealing honestly with such passages—treating them as a genuine part of the biblical witness (but only a part) and giving them the power to bring us up short (but not the character of binding legal pronouncements)—is a difficult and delicate business. And it requires a foundation of trust within the congregation, and between congregation and pastor, that is not quickly or easily established.

As a preacher, one must earn the right to lead people into such deep waters, earn it by faithful service, consistent personal presence, and the demonstrated ability to learn as well as to teach, to listen as well as to speak. Especially for the group that encounters the church and its ministry almost exclusively though weekly worship, this will happen slowly. It will take time and patience—*real* patience, not merely biding your time until you can sail in and set things straight! The points of greatest challenge are not where effective leadership begins and not where you should go before the trust of the community is fairly earned and well deserved. And even where there is a solid foundation, the pulpit is not usually the best place from which to begin delving into difficult or controversial material, particularly if that material may be expected to raise strong personal feelings or sharp disagreement within the congregation. It is generally better to raise such matters first in a setting that allows for an immediate response, one that is as public as the pastor's own voice. There may be other considerations that lead you to choose the sermon as the best way to bring morally challenging, perplexing, or troubling passages before the community, including the fact that it is sometimes the only effective way to speak to the congregation as a whole. But at a minimum, there should be some preparation for such preaching and an opportunity for congregants to express reaction or disagreement as soon after the fact as possible. Later in the chapter I will return to these and other such practical suggestions about preaching on morally difficult texts or topics.

But one more thing must be present if you as a pastor are to use the pulpit to present the stunning demands of the gospel and the high cost of discipleship, if you are to undertake to respond to the passages that offend our moral sensibilities or to the issues that divide us. You must actually love the people entrusted to your care and nurture. This is easier to pay lip service to than to do, and is also easy to deceive yourself about. Love is here understood as combining deep commitment to the other's well-being, regarding each parishioner you confront as one for whom Christ died, one called into free and responsible union with God and the saints. This is essential. Without it, it is not possible to avoid condescension, self-righteousness, and all the temptations that beset anyone who wields the considerable power of the preacher to pronounce upon good and evil. And without it, not only you will suppose that you are always right, but you will also mistakenly suppose that being right about something is sufficient justification for proclaiming it. (It isn't.) Apart from the moral risks to you, in the absence of actual charity, you can be sure that your preaching will not be effective.

I remember a young preacher, perhaps thirty years old at the time, and relatively fresh from a very academically rigorous seminary program. He was smart and gifted and passionate in his convictions, ready (as he thought) to awaken and invigorate the aging suburban congregation that was his first solo assignment. There was the inevitable period of unease and adjustment, as his parishioners tried to accept the leadership of a person half their average age with whom they did not have a great deal in common, politically or otherwise. But by the second year, aided (frankly) by his sweet and patient wife and their two cute little kids, he had made real headway. He had gained the support of at least some of the church's lay leadership and was in a position to accomplish something. And then came the Sunday nearest to Veterans Day that year. It was a day important to many of the older congregants, some who had served in World War II or had fathers and brothers who had served and in some cases died in that conflict. The pastor chose that occasion to preach about the atomic bombing of Hiroshima and Nagasaki by the military forces of the United States, calling it an atrocity and the greatest war crime in history.

The pastor is by no means alone in that judgment. Elizabeth Anscombe, a prominent Roman Catholic moral philosopher of the twentieth century, published an article objecting to an honorary degree granted to President Harry Truman on the grounds that authorizing that attack made him a mass murderer. Many other Christian thinkers, not only pacifists but also those (like Anscombe) who are committed to the just-war tradition, have judged that this act violated the moral constraints on legitimate warfare, both by targeting civilian areas and by unleashing a level of destruction disproportionate to the military objective in view. The point here is not that the preacher's conclusion was necessarily wrong, for that can be hotly debated. The point is that he—at least at that time, in that congregation, in that circumstance—was not entitled to bring that message, even if one supposes him to be correct. He had not shared enough of his congregants' lives and challenges; he had not listened to them enough; he had not worked long or hard enough to deserve their trust; and more than anything, he did not love or respect them nearly enough to be the bearer of that word. The effect of that sermon was predictable. Along with generating outrage, it shattered the bonds that had begun to form, bonds that over time might have made a deeper and more challenging moral leadership possible. His ministry in that congregation did not outlast the year.

Why You Can't Avoid Preaching about Ethics

Despite all I have said about the need for preachers to tread carefully into areas of moral depth and complexity, challenging texts and weighty issues cannot be avoided in all circumstances or forever. If you preach in one of the many contexts where a lectionary governs what verses are read in church from week to week, then the Scriptures that your parishioners hear in worship are at least present in the room. For instance, parts of the Sermon on the Mount (Matt. 5–7), with its astonishing demands to bless your persecutors (5:44) and take no thought for tomorrow's food or clothing (6:25–26), are read every year in the Revised Common Lectionary. Even in denominations that leave the choice of texts to the preacher, it is hard to get through the story of Jesus's birth without running into the story of the slaughter of the innocents (Matt. 2:16–18), with its matter-of-fact depiction of the brutal lengths to which power will go to protect itself. And no matter how hard we try, there is no plausible way to the celebration of the resurrection except through the disturbing narrative of the crucifixion. It is a remarkably timely story about the failure of religious leaders, the triumph of political expediency, and the popularity of torture as a tool of state security. You can avoid addressing or even mentioning any particular passage in your sermon. But if you do, then you must be aware that your silence may be speaking nevertheless. As I suggested earlier, what the pastor never talks about carries ethical lessons too, a confusing and contradictory chorus parishioners are left to interpret on their own: "Bad!" or "Shameful!"; "Not to be questioned!" or "Too hot to handle!"; or perhaps worst of all, "Nothing to do with religion!"

Beyond the provocations presented by lectionary texts or the passages associated with various seasons of the church year, there are events that occur within the life of a congregation or a community that cry out for some response, however halting. A toddler dies in a tragic accident due to a parent's momentary inattention. A trusted member of the community is arrested for child molestation. A person everyone cherishes for his contributions to worship and mission seeks to have his same-sex union celebrated in the church, and the congregation is painfully divided over the faithful response. Or, as has happened repeatedly over the season in which I write this, some promising young life is taken in a confrontation with police where the use of deadly force seems, at best, to have been hasty and excessive. To say nothing at such times is to do more than miss an opportunity; it is to leave parishioners with no help at all in bringing the world of the text and the world they must inhabit together. Your silence could even suggest that the faith you proclaim has nothing to say to frustration and grief, outrage and perplexity. This is a disservice to your people, surely, but it is also a disservice to your religion and an evasion of your calling to serve your congregation in days of darkness as well as light.

And then there are the national and global catastrophes, both natural disasters and those with causes that are all too human. When a hillside in Guatemala collapses after a week of heavy rains, obliterating an entire village and all its inhabitants; when an undersea earthquake spawns a tidal wave that sweeps across hundreds or thousands of miles, carrying uncountable thousands out to sea in a moment; when a group of people, persuaded that the wrongs to their community require blood vengeance against a whole nation, blow up an airliner or send poison gas through a subway—what are we to do with our helplessness and despair, our rage and desire for revenge, with doubt and the temptation to see the whole of life as some kind of savage joke? Who is to blame, and how can we possibly find or trust God in the midst of such random suffering? What is the shape of compassion here, and of justice? All of these are profound moral and theological questions. If they cannot be asked in church, cannot even be named there, then we have reduced our faith to a shallow diversion, unequipped to strengthen or sustain us when we are most desperate and lost.[1]

On such occasions, the hard questions and the hard passages are pressed upon us. To be faithful in such circumstances we must venture some word, even though we may fear that we are altogether out of our depth and may know we have no answers to offer. It is better to face the moral challenges head on—to name the questions with all of their poignancy and pain, even if we can go no further—than to ignore them. We can have confidence that it is safe to do this because we stand in a long line of people, people of profound faith and intimate experience of God, who were brought up short by demands they did not know how to meet and tests of faithfulness they could not master. They were confronted with their own failures until they were certain God had turned from them forever. They were pressed down by experiences of suffering and loss, by betrayal and the collapse of hope, until God seemed unreachable or unreal, or worst of all, simply unconcerned. They faced guilt and fear, doubt and despair, rage and perplexity. And we know all this because the testimony of their struggles runs through the whole body of writings we call the biblical canon, the measure of Christian faith and practice.

We read that testimony in the complaint of Moses against the Israelites who tax him beyond his strength (Num. 11:11–15) and in the desperate plea of Jeremiah that God would speak to him no more words of terror and destruction (Jer. 20:8–9). We find it in the protest of Job, who cannot understand wherein he has

---

1. For a powerful and convincing account of the church's need to recover the biblical resources of lament in its liturgy and preaching, see Sally Brown and Patrick Miller's wonderful anthology *Lament: Reclaiming Practices in Pulpit, Pew, and Public Square* (Louisville: Westminster John Knox, 2005), especially the essays by C. Clifton Black and Peter J. Paris.

offended God (Job 10:2–7), and we see it woven like a dark thread
through the many psalms of lament that implore rescue from a
God who seems to have gone deaf and silent (e.g., Pss. 6; 10; 42;
44; 88). We hear it raw in psalms of imprecation that scream for
the destruction of enemies—and for revenge (e.g., Pss. 35; 69; 74;
137). And as Christians, we hear it echo down the ages from the
cross, where God's own Son cries out the psalmist's desperate
question: "My God, why have you forsaken me?" (Matt. 27:46;
Ps. 22:1). Here we see that no question born of real anguish is
finally out of bounds, and the difference between faith and unbelief at such times may be no more than this: that when we cry
out in grief, in perplexity, in doubt or anger or despair, we know
the One to whom we speak. And we wait for an answer, perhaps
hoping against hope, supported by the faith of others when, for
a time at least, our own faith is battered or gone.

But it is not only the provocations of the lectionary or the events
that threaten to shatter us that make it necessary sometimes to
speak of what is difficult. We cannot avoid the demands of Scripture
that challenge our lives, the passages that affront our sensibilities,
or the issues that confuse and divide us, because to do so would
require that we dramatically edit the Word that we have been given
to proclaim. It would mean not merely ignoring individual passages but effectively rewriting the central text of our faith, where
barely two pages into the narrative, the first peace of creation is
destroyed. Human communion with the Creator is broken, as the
mysterious figure of the serpent prompts rebellion, exploiting an
ignorance made dangerous by pride. The whole of the complex
and many-layered recital of Scripture is driven by the consequences
of that rupture, a tale of human efforts to live apart from God and
of God's initiatives to repair the breach. The covenant with Noah,
the calling of Abraham, the rescue from Egypt and the gift of the
law, the ever-rejected and ever-renewed calls of the prophets—all
are part of the overarching story of God's redemptive work.

It is a story full of failures and disasters as well as dramatic
rescues, all of them evidence of God's abiding faithfulness and

unrelenting determination to reclaim and restore creation. It is in this context, and only here, that the compressed affirmation we know as the Apostles' Creed makes sense, testifying to God's remedy for a malady that cannot otherwise be acknowledged or understood. Unpopular as it may be in an age where we are so accustomed to the evasion of responsibility, the gospel of Christ is the good news about God's response to evil in all its dimensions. It encompasses not only the particular acts of malice or greed, cowardice or deception that we commit, but also the experience of sin as a condition, a burden, and a kind of captivity. As preachers, we must confront the demands of holiness and our perennial failure to meet them because this confrontation is at the heart of our confession, and God's answer to it is at the center of our proclamation. In the arresting phrase of Barbara Brown Taylor, "Sin is our only hope,"[2] because acknowledging our brokenness and our inability to heal ourselves is the start of the only road home.[3]

But even for those willing to accept the Bible's fundamental theological account of sin as not merely a problem we have but as a reality that somehow has us, enormous challenges remain. Seeking moral insight and guidance from a collection of ancient texts means reckoning with the substantial differences among them, as well as the dramatic differences between their material and social world and the one we inhabit. This is part of the complexity that makes the moral interpretation of Scripture so contested. This also makes it tempting to avoid at all costs dealing with discomforting passages and controversial issues from the pulpit (or indeed, if possible, anywhere else). But the costs of doing so are high, for to take this course is to denature the church, stripping away its character as a community of moral conversation, moral discernment, and

2. Barbara Brown Taylor, *Speaking of Sin: The Lost Language of Salvation* (Cambridge, MA: Cowley, 2000), 41. This is a brief and wonderful book, offering a richly nuanced treatment that remains accessible to general readers.

3. For an old but remarkably applicable argument for the spiritual necessity of claiming responsibility for our own actions, see Phillips Brooks's 1883 sermon "The Fire and the Calf," http://www.christianity9to5.org/the-fire-and-the-calf.

moral formation. This leaves a church body incapable of shaping its members in faithfulness and thus unable to fulfill its most basic social mission, which is to serve as a contrast community, a sign of the in-breaking reign of God.

This is not only, or even chiefly, a loss for the church; it is also a loss for the world for whose sake the church exists and is called out, because it saps the power of evangelism. It is still possible, of course, to announce the good news, to say in public that the time has come when God will save God's people. But in the absence of the church as a genuine and distinctive moral community, such speech is profoundly undermined. Not only the persuasiveness but even the intelligibility of the gospel *depends* upon a community that embodies its claim that God has made a new way of life possible and founded a society in which power is *power for* and not merely *power over* other human beings. The ancient fathers declared that persecution could not prevent the spread of the faith, for "the blood of Christians is seed for the Church."[4] A modern commentator has similarly argued that the lives of the saints are the essential evidence of our faith.[5] In life and in death, the church exists to bear witness not merely by what we say but by what we do and who we are. For this reason, the hard work of moral formation cannot be sidestepped.

I have tried to offer a balanced account of the risks, and also the sometime necessity, of preaching on the most demanding or troubling of biblical texts and of addressing from the pulpit the moral issues that perplex and divide our churches. I have argued for the importance of naming the things we would rather avoid, the reality of evil, including our frequent complicity in it, as well as the depth of suffering it brings upon us and others. Having encouraged you to venture into such challenging territory, I will try to offer some guidance for the undertaking. These can be only generalities, meant to offer you the fruit of my own and others'

4. Tertullian, *Apologeticus* 50; translation mine.
5. See Stanley Hauerwas, *A Community of Character: Toward a Constructive Christian Social Ethic* (Notre Dame, IN: University of Notre Dame Press, 1981), 92.

experience and observation. In the end, it will be your own insight and judgment that shape your proclamation, and your own prayer that supports it and (with the power and help of the Holy Spirit) determines its effectiveness.

Some Guidance for the Venture

In the preceding discussion, I have moved freely among various kinds of ethical difficulty that may be presented by biblical texts or by the circumstances in which proclamation must be offered. But while there is some overlap in the way in which different kinds of preaching challenges may be approached, there are also distinctions, strategies that are applicable to one situation but not another, and missteps that are especially important to avoid on a particular occasion. For the purpose of clarifying what counsel is being offered for a given sort of challenge, I will divide this section of practical guidance into four categories: (1) responding to events that raise issues about evil and suffering, (2) responding to biblical texts that are morally appealing but seem too difficult for us, (3) grappling with texts that seem morally problematic or troubling, and (4) dealing with passages or issues that are controversial and divisive in the church. It only remains to note that sometimes a single passage or issue presents more than one kind of difficulty or is experienced quite differently by various members of the congregation. In such cases it may be necessary to acknowledge the complexity and to address different dimensions of the problem separately.

Preaching in the Face of Disaster

Nearly all Americans who had reached the age of six by September 2001 can tell you where they were and what they were doing on the eleventh when they heard about the attacks on the World Trade Center and the Pentagon. Coverage of those events utterly saturated the broadcast media and internet outlets for days on end. Shock and grief and outrage gathered strangers in public spaces to weep and to express their determination to unite in response to the assault upon their nation. By the end of that week, most Americans had seen many times the television footage of planes striking the Twin Towers, the pictures of trapped workers jumping to their deaths, and the shots of first responders pulling the bodies of victims from the shattered wall of the Pentagon. They had stared at the crash site in Pennsylvania where passengers had brought down their own airliner rather than letting it become a weapon. The images, at once horrifying and mesmerizing, played over and over again, until they were burned into our brains. By Sunday morning, initial shock had given way to a whole range of conflicting emotions, and people of faith (and many of no particular faith) gathered in churches for mutual support and to see what solace and direction Christian faith might have to offer.

Preachers responded to this occasion in a great variety of ways. Many looked to the history of Israel with its long saga of national catastrophes for words and images to express the nation's grief and rage. Others turned to the Psalter, the incomparable prayer book of God's people across millennia. Some sought to interpret the geopolitical situation, explaining what actions and policies had generated such hatred toward America and its people. A minority of preachers undertook to identify the sinners who had offended God and caused the withdrawal of divine protection from the nation (though they did not all agree in their identification). Some drew upon the theological and liturgical traditions of the church and offered words of reassurance and confidence that God could and would comfort and heal those who were suffering. A few, astonishingly, simply kept to the sermon as planned before the attacks, perhaps adding prayers for the injured and grieving to the order of worship. Presumably, not knowing what to say, they thought it safest to say nothing in particular.

To begin with the obvious, there exists no single right approach to preaching after an event of this magnitude and no one faithful message to deliver on what was, for Americans, an occasion without precedent. Indeed, there may be *no* right thing to say after such a disaster. It may well be that the best response for a preacher in the short term would be to lead a profound and patient time of silence to express our unanswerable questions and our unassuageable grief. Even Job's comforters sat in silence for seven days and nights, "for they saw that his suffering was very great" (Job 2:13), and they only incurred God's anger after they spoke. There are, however, *wrong* approaches, things that are wrong to do because they increase suffering unnecessarily, or even more fundamentally wrong because they present an understanding of the world basically at odds with the gospel Christian preachers are authorized to proclaim. And there are certainly messages that, even if theologically correct, cannot be offered at a particular time or place or to a particular community, at least not otherwise than in response to a direct call from God. (If the Almighty should be pleased to give you a word of judgment or conviction to declare to the victims of a disaster, then do so. And please accept my condolences, for it is grievous work. But before you dare to announce "thus saith the LORD," be aware that in the texts of prophecy, the penalties that fall upon self-appointed prophets are harsh indeed.)

Beyond general suggestions, a great deal depends upon particular context: the congregation you are given to care for and the relationship you have developed with them to that point. For pastors in New York and Washington, DC, after 9/11 everything was set against the backdrop of particular losses as they sat with the spouses, children, parents, and friends of the victims and dealt with raw and overwhelming pain. For those at greater distances, it was an occasion to talk about evil and rage and how to live in a world where human beings can inflict such devastation upon one another. For much of the time after a tragedy of whatever scale, at the side of the grieving, the perplexed, and those whose lives are newly shattered, the wisest course is to stay close, listen hard, and pray constantly. The following seven general guidelines, many concerning things *not* to do, are offered for when Sunday worship comes around and your community turns to you to speak, somehow, the word of God's presence into what seems an abyss.

(1) Don't say nothing. That is, do not ignore the circumstance, pretend nothing has happened, or try to somehow bracket off from worship the one thing that fills everyone's minds. If there are no words, at least name the event that stuns us to silence, and let the silence last until it carries our shock and sense of emptiness.

(2) Don't offer an explanation. When something terrible happens, it is deeply ingrained in us to search for a reason: something that caused this event or that might have gone differently and prevented it. This is chiefly to assure ourselves that there is some intelligible order in the universe and to hold at bay the fearful idea that violence or illness or accident can be so utterly random. But yielding to this impulse only denies the vulnerability that we all share by offering a false reassurance. It may also increase the suffering of actual victims, who are likely already to torment themselves with regrets: "If only . . ."

(3) Don't try to fix blame, either human or cosmic. This is a special case of the previous advice, stressed here because it is particularly important. As a pastor, your office is neither to decide who is at fault nor to try to "justify the ways of God to man," in the memorable but arrogant phrase of John Milton.[6] Unless you are prompted by a special revelation that compels you to speak (see the above warning about prophecy), it is presumptuous to suppose that God's purposes, or even the complex web of motives and circumstances that govern human acts, can be read backward from the transcript of events.

(4) Don't pretend to have clarity, certainty, or resignation you do not really possess. As a preacher, you need to control your own emotions in order to speak, and to avoid the appearance of manipulation. (The pulpit is not the place from which to seek your own consolation.) But do not hide or deny your own feelings

6. John Milton, *Paradise Lost* (New York: Norton, 2005), 1.26. Here is one of the places where one suspects that Milton was perhaps a better poet than theologian.

either, assuming a posture somehow above the pain and confusion of the time at hand. Knowing theoretically that "all things work together for good for those who love God" (Rom. 8:28) does not mean that we can feel that in the face of catastrophe, or even say it with a straight face. Real resignation to the will of God is a virtue won at length by those far advanced in holiness, and it is won through struggle, not by evading it.

(5) Make space in the gathered community for the full reach of emotions and the whole range of responses. When grief is new, shock still resonating, and people are trying to come to terms with some unimaginable new reality, there must be room for all the things people are feeling: the frightening and troubling outbursts of rage and despair as well as the orthodox expressions of acceptance and trust and confidence in God's power to heal. To exclude those whose suffering drives them to question and doubt, or to silence their protests, is only to force those emotions underground and to isolate people at their time of greatest need. It also substitutes a shallow and impoverished understanding of our relationship with God in place of the model offered in Scripture, where we are invited to cry out our deepest grief and pour out our hearts without reserve.

(6) Use the common resources of text, tradition, and liturgy. In times of profound loss, confusion, and pain, familiarity is powerful. It carries us when we are past thinking and beyond forming words. The most frequently heard stories, best-known hymns, most-often-repeated prayers or affirmations can touch us where no degree of eloquence can reach, even when we are hardly aware of what we are saying. There is a reason Psalm 23 is so often invoked by people in sorrow or fear: the things we know "by heart" can steady us when the mind is still reeling.

(7) Tell the truth. This is really the underlying ground of all that has gone before, and here it includes not only the state of

your own heart and mind, but the true experience of those most affected by the event. It is also the hardest advice to follow when the truth seems like more than we dare to admit. It might seem safer to say what we think we and others *should* believe, feel, or think, or to quote one of the many Bible verses that affirm the absolute security of those who rest in God's hand, from which no disaster can snatch them. These are statements of the deepest truth, of course, and the ability to rest upon such affirmations when pain engulfs us is one of the richest fruits of faith long and securely held. But very few of us can immediately respond to devastating loss like Job: "The LORD gave, and the LORD has taken away; blessed be the name of the LORD" (Job 1:21). In the meantime, on our way to the perfect serenity of the saints, we must not encourage people to lie in prayer, a practice both futile and unnecessary. God, who has heard his own Son cry out his despair, can bear with our anguish and walk with us through the darkness. It is often the only road back to trust.

Preaching the High Demands of the Kingdom

Thirty-some years ago, I was staying with a friend who lived on the Connecticut coastline. On Sunday morning I went with her to the local Congregational church, a lovely white-steepled structure, the very image of old New England piety. The pastor was a man of early middle age, with a thin face and a balding head, and the only minister I have ever seen in person who still wore the old Geneva tab collar common among Calvinist ministers of an earlier era. He looked for all the world like he had stepped out of a nineteenth-century portrait. I confess that I did not expect much of his preaching.

His church followed the lectionary, and when he stood in the pulpit he dutifully read aloud the assigned gospel text for the day, which was Mark 10:17–27. It is the passage we commonly call "the story of the rich young ruler," though that phrase is a composite description drawn from all three Synoptic Gospels. When he had finished the reading, including the directive that the man who desired to inherit eternal life sell all that he possessed to come follow Jesus, the preacher closed the Bible and looked directly at his congregation. He began to speak: "Let's face it, brothers and sisters, this is one of the things we all wish Jesus hadn't said." I think my mouth probably fell open. I had never heard anyone be so utterly blunt from the pulpit about what almost everyone in the room secretly felt. It wasn't a great leap of insight on his part, of course; we were gathered in the town of Essex, home of the Connecticut Yacht Club, where houses started at seven figures even in the 1980s. Radical dispossession was sure to be a tough sell. I just didn't expect anyone to admit it right up front like that.

The preacher went on to walk with us through the passage, with its central invitation to life and its sad ending, where the man went away grieving, "for he had many possessions" (Mark 10:22). He talked about what was at stake, but also about how utterly unreasonable such counsel seemed to us, how impossible even to take it seriously. And he talked gently about what it might be like to take small steps toward being unbound from all that we owned so that we might more closely follow Jesus. There was no demand, no threat, and no separation between the preacher and his congregation—just the suggestion, that we might begin together a journey toward trusting less in our possessions and more in God by giving away some of what we had to those whose need, was great. The worship service ended with a hymn and a benediction, and we all left quietly. It was one of the best lessons on preaching I ever got. This was not so much for its conclusion, though there was wisdom in that as well, but for the honesty with which he confronted the distance between the texts we call Scripture and our own minds and hearts.[7]

The sermon text above is one of a set of passages familiar to any preacher as "the hard sayings of Jesus," pronouncements scattered

---

7. For my own moral interpretation of this gospel text, see Sondra Ely Wheeler, *Wealth as Peril and Obligation: The New Testament on Possessions* (Grand Rapids: Eerdmans, 1993), chap. 3.

throughout the Gospels on the demands of discipleship and the requirements of righteousness that seem impossibly out of our reach. Matthew 5–7 and Luke 6 offer a rich sampling. They are joined by similar teachings of the apostles: Paul's admonitions to pray for persecutors, forswear revenge, and feed and care for enemies (Rom. 12:14–20); Peter's invitation to rejoice in the trials that test and purify your faith (1 Pet. 1:6–7); John's announcement that no one who lives in Christ sins, and no one guilty of sin can claim to know him (1 John 3:4–6). Nor are such calls to charity and holiness confined to the New Testament. Hebrew Scripture is the original source of the central and defining demands that we are to love God with our whole heart (Deut. 6:4–5) and our neighbors as ourselves (Lev. 19:18), which Jesus quotes when asked about the greatest commandment (Matt. 22:35–40 and parallels). And love as understood in the Old Testament is both active and interventionist. It includes providing for the needy, whether kindred or stranger (Lev. 19:10, 33–34), as well as reaching out to help those endangered by others. The Good Samaritan of Jesus's parable, it turns out, is merely obeying the law: "You shall not stand idly by your neighbor's blood" (Lev. 19:16, my translation). Many other examples could be offered, but these will serve to illustrate the point.

Capped by "Be perfect, therefore, as your heavenly Father is perfect" (Matt. 5:48), such passages are at the same time terrifying and beautiful. Even when we cannot imagine living our lives according to their rigorous standards, neither can anyone who is captured by their vision of mirroring the goodness of God desire simply to leave them behind. What are we to do with such extraordinary demands? What are we to say about them? Once again, in the following seven points I offer only general advice, consisting as much of things to avoid as of things to do. The substance of what a preacher must say depends upon particular context and conviction, on a reading of the world as well as of the text, and on the kind of relationship she or he has developed with the congregation.

(1) Acknowledge the difficulty. Do not ignore the stunning character of such texts, or by silence imply that you or your listeners are eagerly absorbing these directives and are ready to go out and love your enemies (Matt. 5:44), forgo the pursuit of food and clothing (Luke 12:22), and lay down your lives for the sake of your sisters and brothers (1 John 3:16). Like lying in prayer, dissembling in the pulpit can serve no purpose. God is not fooled, and it presents a terrible model.

(2) Heighten rather than reduce the tension. Do not try to soft-pedal the challenge by playing down the seriousness of the demand or the distance between what seems reasonable and possible to us and what the text seems to say. Instead, name and underscore that distance, so that your most skeptical listener hears his or her own doubt or disbelief acknowledged in your words.

(3) Show how the gospel that Christians profess makes these moral demands intelligible. Once we've approached the text from the standpoint of our own culture and its account of what is true, it is time to look at it from the perspective of Christian faith and its claims. What difference does it make if we suppose for a moment that the affirmations we routinely make in church—that God alone is the source of all safety and blessing, that those who seek God's reign and righteousness will be given what they need, that God's love is eternal and cannot be thwarted by death—are actually true? How would the unreasonable advice and the impossible demands of Scripture make sense to us if we took these statements as descriptions of reality?

(4) Explore the connection between Christian faith and the possibility of being morally formed by the demands of Scripture. Considering the passage from the standpoint of the gospel can help us to see how the degrees of faith we have might enable us to respond in some fashion to its call. If we believe that God cares for us, we become able to let down some of our own defenses. If we

can venture to trust that God will provide for our basic needs as we pursue justice, we may find ourselves equipped to live with less anxiety and greater integrity. Recognizing that Christian hope is properly located not in staving off death but in resurrection can free us to live with more courage and joy, even in the face of real threats.

(5) Affirm God's eagerness to bless even a flicker of desire in the right direction and the importance and fruitfulness of beginning the journey even in a small way. In the face of profound challenges and calls for dramatic transformation, there is comfort in the promises of Isaiah regarding the gentle determination of God's chosen servant:

> I have put my spirit upon him;
>   he will bring forth justice to the nations.
> He will not cry or lift up his voice,
>   or make it heard in the street;
> a bruised reed he will not break,
>   and a dimly burning wick he will not quench;
>   he will faithfully bring forth justice.
> He will not grow faint or be crushed
>   until he has established justice in the earth.
>   Isaiah 42:1–4

Dimly burning wicks though we are, we rest in the confidence that our pursuit of holiness and justice is met and sustained by the Spirit of God, and we trust that no step, however small and halting, will be scorned. We may find ourselves lacking the faith to imitate the apostles who left everything to follow Jesus, or the singleness of heart of the great saints of the church who abandoned the life they knew to devote themselves entirely to works of mercy. We are unlikely to be able to make a standing long jump into the perfection of charity we are invited to attain. But we can begin in some way on the path toward greater faithfulness, and that beginning is of enormous importance. It gives us a taste of what it means to share God's life in the world more deeply. Thus we are drawn into the joyful work of bringing forth justice, as Jesus meets us in the hungry, the oppressed, and the imprisoned whom we serve.

(6) Invite your congregation to pray together for grace, if not to wholeheartedly embrace God's will, then to at least want to do so. Sometimes it is difficult even to imagine what it would mean to take the high demands of discipleship seriously, or how to start. Other times it is easy enough to imagine—but altogether too daunting to do. We can hardly pray as Jesus taught us with a straight face because we know full well that we are not ready for God's will to be done in our own lives. Here as elsewhere, honesty is vital. It is better to say, "God help us, for we do not trust you enough to take this step," than to gloss over the fact with a rousing chorus of "Just a Closer Walk with Thee." If we cannot honestly pray that we do want God's will in our lives, perhaps we can pray to want it—or failing that, to *want* to want it!

(7) Remind your community that the work of inward transformation is not ours but God's. Our part in this work is to steadily show up, in season and out of it, counting on God, "for it is God who is at work in you, enabling you both to will and to work for his good pleasure" (Phil. 2:13). Faithfulness in Christian life does not come from moral striving and effort so much as from the inward gifts of faith, hope, and love that allow us to live lives of generosity and trust. These must be shaped in us by the Holy Spirit, through all the ordinary disciplines of our shared lives: worship and service, prayer and fasting, sorrows and celebrations. A colleague of mine once suggested, half in jest, that we might all find ourselves before the throne of God someday having to explain, "We could not obey your commands because we did not believe your promises." For most of us, the truth is more muddled. Like the man who appeals to Jesus to heal his son, we have to say "I believe; help my unbelief!" (Mark 9:24). Church is where we come together, week after week, in order that God might help our unbelief and shape us into people capable of faithfulness.

Preaching on Troubling Texts

In the last section, I talked about texts that are morally difficult because they call on us to display a degree of mercy, generosity, or single-hearted devotion that we do not possess. Texts commanding us to turn the other cheek, love our enemies, and give all to the poor are challenging because we don't live such lives, and (if we are honest) do not really want to. Nevertheless, we glimpse in such directives a form of life that is beautiful and admirable, even if we cannot imagine actually embracing it; at least some of the time, we feel that we ought to. These are "hard sayings" only in that we find ourselves unable—or perhaps simply unwilling—to act upon them. Now we move to talk about a different kind of difficulty: texts that are hard in quite another sense because they strike us as morally problematic, troubling, or simply wrong. (For the time being, I will leave to one side texts that are seen as problematic by some but are affirmed by others in the same community as genuine norms. These I will take up under the heading of texts and topics that are the source of moral controversy. Of course, which texts belong in this category depends on what community you are in.)

Some passages, such as those that flatly forbid divorce or use "immorality" as the only category for nonmarital sex, may be morally confusing to contemporary readers because we are not convinced that they are right or that we should try to live accordingly. Other texts, such as those counseling the subordination of women or the obedience of slaves, may be morally offensive because many of us are convinced they are wrong and that we *shouldn't* live in accord with them. Finally, texts that call down and seem even to celebrate the vengeance of God upon wrongdoers, such as the psalms of imprecation (Pss. 58; 59; 69; 137) or some prophetic denunciations (Isa. 10; Jer. 6; Ezek. 29; Hosea 9), may shock our sensibilities. They also confuse our understanding of who God is. If anything, passages that are morally troubling in these ways are addressed in church even less often than those that call on us to cast away our possessions or lay down our lives. But our strategy of avoidance is not sustainable. Either we give up the power of the biblical canon to form the church, or we retain its power only by vigorous (and mostly unacknowledged) editing. And then, of course, it is the editor who has the power rather than the canon of Scripture.

Because the church is a community gathered around a story told uniquely in the Bible, it must grapple with passages that challenge our assumptions and call our judgments into question. We have to seek to understand the biblical texts that affront us and be willing to wrestle with texts and ideas that offend our own moral standards. This is not by any means to say that all other judgments and sources of insight must yield in the face of any single verse or even any single canonical source. For one thing, neither the Bible as a whole nor even the New Testament taken alone displays the kind of unanimity on every topic that would allow a single passage or author to stand as an unimpeachable and final source of moral authority. The principle that Scripture must interpret Scripture is old and well established. So is the idea that texts must be read for the purpose and intent of the writer and in light of the context and understanding of those addressed. In reckoning with morally troubling texts, we need to use all the resources at hand to understand why the particular text says what it does, what its place is in the wider work of which it is part, and what its theological significance and purpose might be. These resources will include the insights of cultural history and the tools of historical criticism, as well as the perspectives of readers of different backgrounds and circumstances.

Drawing upon all of these will put us in a position to read with insight and sympathy, both of which are necessary for any genuine critical treatment of an ancient text. Such study may lead us to reinterpret or reconsider the moral import of a passage or even to decide that it rests upon assumptions we cannot share and offers directives we should not follow. But we must also be willing to let Scripture confront and challenge the morality of our own day, as it so often challenged the morality of the times and places in

which it was written and received. To do otherwise is to decide in
advance that the Bible is not allowed to teach us anything about
life in light of the gospel that we do not already know. The eight
guidelines below offer some approaches to talking about passages
we find morally troubling. Which ones are appropriate in any
particular case will depend upon the community you serve and
the kind of difficulty the text presents.

(1) *Acknowledge the difficulty the text creates for your listeners.*
As in the case of morally challenging texts, it is important to name
the inward response you may expect your congregation to have and
to be candid about the degree to which you share it. To do so is
part of taking both the text and the moral understanding of your
community seriously.

(2) *Underscore rather than minimize the disparity between the
moral assumptions of the writer and our own views.* You want
those who are most confused or troubled by the text to be confi-
dent that you understand their reaction, which may range from
uncertainty to dismay to flat rejection. Whether or not your own
response matches the most extreme response of your congregants,
you need to reflect and reckon with their reaction in how you
engage the reading.

(3) *Provide as much historical and cultural context as you
can to help your congregation hear the text with sympathy and
understanding.* Here is where the training gained in your formal
preparation for ministry comes most directly into play. Sharing
your knowledge about the writers and original readers of the
text, understanding something of the circumstances that they
confronted and the world of ideas in which they were formed,
can help to make sense of things that are alien and off-putting.
The point here is not simply to draw contrasts between then and
now that will justify dismissing the passage as having no moral
relevance; that would require far more substantial consideration.

Rather, the initial goal is to seek to understand the context and meaning of the passage as it was originally written, long before it was adopted by the church as Scripture.

(4) Remind congregants of the character, purpose, and genre of the text in view. When looking at texts that raise moral problems for contemporary readers, remember that the biblical writers were not writing systematic "ethics" in our modern sense. The Old Testament is a collection of books drawn from diverse sources and settings and compiled across centuries. It includes history and poetry, proverbs and stories, law and prophecy. It is morally rich, instructive, and powerful as well as sometimes disturbing, but at no point is it a treatise in ethics. Likewise, the various writers of the epistles were giving young Christian communities instruction in their new faith and guidance in living it out in contexts that were often hostile. And the writers of the Gospels and Acts were handing on the story and significance of the central events that brought those communities into being and gave them their identity. Biblical texts, like all texts, deserve to be read in light of the genre to which they belong.

(5) Explore with your congregation the purpose or aim of the text within the larger work of which it is part. Since even the direct moral imperatives of the Bible are embedded in larger narratives or theological expositions, it is necessary to look beyond the particular passage to the wider literary setting, its place in an argument or its function in a story. How does this passage fit into the writer's broader agenda, and what purpose does it serve there? What is the theological point in view, and how does the specifically moral teaching contribute to that point? To what extent is the particular instruction simply an example or sign whose place might be taken by another, and to what extent is the particular teaching itself the point?[8]

8. E.g., compare the instruction to go two miles with the person who compels you to go one (a regular imposition of Roman soldiers on occupied peoples) with the

(6) Having the historical setting and the evident theological purpose in view, consider what difference a dramatically altered context might make. Sometimes the purpose for which a specific act seems to be recommended can no longer be well served by that action. To take a simple example, Jesus's command that the disciples imitate him in washing one another's feet (John 13:14) is in some Christian traditions taken as a basis for a continuing practice of ritual foot washing. This may be a perfectly legitimate liturgical adaptation of the text. But we might also look for different forms of necessary but menial service to perform for our sisters and brothers in our own setting, where roads are likely to be paved and people wear shoes. To be comparable to washing feet, a task performed at the time by slaves, it would need to be something ordinarily done by unskilled and poorly paid workers—or by one of the legions of mostly female caregivers who provide unpaid service to sick and elderly relatives. We could consider volunteering to scrub toilets or empty bedpans for those in need and perhaps come closer to the spirit of "do as I have done to you" (John 13:15).

(7) Reason forward from the broader context and the apparent intent to the behavior that would serve that purpose in the contemporary world. A similar strategy might be employed regarding Paul's complicated argument concerning women covering their heads when praying or prophesying in church (1 Cor. 11:2–16).[9] The surrounding passages suggest Paul's chief concern is that Christians should do nothing to undermine the appeal and per-

---

admonition to love your enemies, Matt. 5:41 and 5:44, respectively. It is easy to see how the former is merely a particular instance of the latter and is not proposed as a rule for all time. It is harder to argue that the admonition to love enemies is similarly context-dependent, though some have tried. For a more fully detailed proposal about the moral interpretation and appropriation of New Testament texts, see Wheeler, *Wealth as Peril and Obligation*, chap. 7.

9. This is a perplexing passage in many ways, including how it seems to contradict what Paul says a few chapters later concerning women praying, prophesying, or speaking in church (1 Cor. 14:33–35). This has led some scholars to suggest that it is a later interpolation into the letter; without taking a position on this question, we will work with the canonical version.

suasiveness of the gospel they preach. Writing in a cultural setting where only prostitutes and women of questionable moral character appeared in public with their heads uncovered, he seems to be seeking to avoid scandalizing local custom and bringing suspicion on the church. Of course, in the contemporary Western setting we have no such custom to honor. A woman wearing a head covering in church today will not be seen as displaying respectful deference to authority but will merely look odd or stylish, depending on whether she chooses a veil or a fashionable hat. This does not mean that there is no possibility of offending the moral views of our contemporaries regarding the treatment of women. In fact, it is not uncommon to hear people outside the church express disdain for what they view as the sexism and gender discrimination that persist within the church and its institutions. Whether this charge has merit is a complex matter, but in any case it raises the question: What kind of behavior toward women would we embrace if our aim was to avoid placing stumbling blocks in the way of our contemporaries?

(8) Be honest about unresolved questions, whatever they are. There is power in speaking the truth, even when the truth is "God, help us, for we don't know what to do with this passage." It puts us in a position to wrestle with the canon of Scripture as it actually is—a book by various authors addressing different questions in diverse contexts, a complex witness that sometimes brings us up short—rather than relying on a harmonized and sanitized construction of our own invention. It is better to be candid about our confusion or our dismay than to make a bow in the direction of "biblical authority" without any clarity or conviction about what that should mean.

Preaching on Morally Controversial Texts or Topics

There are excellent reasons to want to avoid addressing subjects that are likely to create moral conflict and division in the community. Whether it concerns matters of public policy, church life and leadership, or standards of personal behavior, ethical disagreements can easily become toxic and destructive. When differences in understanding and judgment are linked to the conviction that those who disagree are advocating something morally wrong, it quickly becomes difficult to continue a real conversation. Once things have gone from discussion to debate, the focus usually shifts from gaining the best insight to proving that your side is right. Positions harden, arguments become repetitive, and, as tempers rise, dialogue may descend into mutual accusation and even name-calling.

Polemics in the church are justified by those who engage in them by the claim of truth. One side may speak confidently of "biblical truth," for instance, while the other side is likely to offer its opposite moral prescriptions under some equally high-sounding rubric like "speaking truth to power." Both sides assume that the truth is pretty simple, that it's all on one side, and that this is *their* side. From this starting point, one need not move too far to assume (like the Spanish Inquisition!) that error can have no rights. It is easy in such circumstances to feel entitled to think and to speak ill of one's opponents and even to treat them quite badly. The temptation is to suppose that strong ethical disagreements about important matters arise because those on the other side are stupid or evil or both. Thus they are not entitled to respect or to a sympathetic hearing.

In reality, disputes about ethics arise for a number of reasons that are rarely as simple as "one side is bad." They arise sometimes because of misunderstanding, where the issue itself or the circumstances affecting it or the likely results of proposed decisions are not fully grasped by one side or, more often, by either side. Such failures of understanding are especially likely when the underlying issue is complicated—for instance, decisions to take military action or strategies for financing health care. Differences may be made more intractable by deliberate misinformation, particularly when the self-interest of some persons or groups shaping the conversation is implicated in the outcome. This is frequently the case in the political arena and sometimes in the area of church leadership as well. Moral conflicts are also made immensely more difficult to navigate by the emotions they engage, whether fear or outrage or frustration or even passionate commitment to a cause. And of course, ethical controversies in the church really are sometimes matters of fundamentally different principle that cannot readily be resolved by careful inquiry and real consideration of the other's viewpoint—though not so often as the participants might think. In such cases, collective prayer and discernment are called for—a course nearly impossible to pursue in the heat of argument.

At root, ethical disagreements arise because the truth about human life is complex and many-sided. And which part of that complexity you see depends upon where you stand, what your experience has been, and what you pay attention to. This makes it difficult for any one person to recognize and take account of everything that might bear on moral judgment, and it is one of the reasons that Christian tradition has located primary responsibility for moral discernment with groups of believers rather than individuals. In addition, the faith we profess adds ethical nuances of its own. It requires us to live our lives poised between the "already" and the "not yet" of Christian conviction, between the truth that God's reign has broken upon the world and that it is not fully realized. It is not always clear where the balance lies in a particular matter, or what the shape of faithfulness might look like in a world awaiting redemption. Already in the first century we see sharp disagreements arise (Acts 6:1), and councils convened to resolve disputes and to settle theological and ethical questions for the sake of church unity (Acts 15). But this strategy requires that the church develop the capacity for thoughtful and fruitful conversations concerning matters we disagree about, rather than evading the issues or imitating the disastrous model of public debate in the twenty-first century.

All this being said, most of the time the pulpit is not the best place to bring up matters likely to be hotly contested within your community because its communication is generally one-way. For those strongly opposed to any view you may express, or those who object to the issue even being raised in church (either because the right answer is "obvious" or because it is too controversial or "political" a subject), preaching on such a topic will seem like an abuse of your role. People who do take offense will have the whole remainder of the service to stew over it and may confront you at the door, too angry to have a useful conversation. Worse yet, they may leave angry and say nothing, making future conversation difficult or impossible. For these reasons, it is generally preferable to take up controversial subjects in a setting where those who disagree or are disturbed by the conversation can express their own response immediately and openly in the community.

Apart from the disadvantages of unilateral communication compared to dialogue, sermons are usually too short to present morally complicated issues in ways that are adequate and fair to more than one point of view. Being oral rather than written, they also give people less opportunity to carefully evaluate the arguments made (or perhaps to refute them). Finally, preaching is not a good way to present a great deal of information—other related passages, details of history, information that might illuminate a moral issue in important ways—even though it may be pertinent. Nevertheless, there are sometimes compelling reasons to talk about a divisive issue in a sermon. Even when there are, though, the pulpit should never be the first and only place where such a subject is raised. It is helpful to provide forewarning of the coming sermon topic and some account of why it seems important to address in this time and place. Opportunities should be offered for feedback and for learning more about the issue and the concerns that various parties have raised. There must be time to listen to one another and to ask questions and safe places to express disagreement or uncertainty. In short, in the midst of our controversies, we must continue to be the church.

Given a broader context, and with careful preparation on the part of the preacher, the treatment of morally contested texts and issues in preaching can be rich and constructive. It may serve the church in its work of formation and also the wider community, which might see in it a model for how to engage respectfully and responsibly those with whom we disagree about important things. And despite the risks involved, there are times when it is vital to speak of controversial and divisive topics in worship: times when events in the life of the congregation or in the wider world introduce an "elephant in the room" that we must either address or pointedly ignore. (The abysmal state of contemporary public and political discourse might itself constitute such an elephant, an occasion on which the church is called upon to name a pressing problem and offer a way forward.) Below are five general guidelines for approaching such controversial texts from the pulpit.

(1) Do not tackle bitterly contested issues in preaching unless your relationship with the congregation is well established and firmly grounded in trust. Even if carefully conducted, conversations in areas of moral disagreement are difficult and often painful. This is one of the areas where a pastor needs to have earned the right to lead the congregation through loving and faithful service and must take great care not to squander that trust.

(2) Consider whether the pulpit is the most appropriate place in which to take up the topic. If there are good reasons for your choice, explain them and, at a minimum, offer opportunities for feedback and open discussion. Provide balanced and factually accurate resources for those who want to pursue the issue.

(3) Use the power of the pulpit with fairness and restraint. The pastor who stands up to preach wields significant power and the implicit authority of the Word of God. But serious moral debates arise because the truth is complicated and is usually to be found on more than one side of an issue. Be extremely careful to present all positions in a controversy in such a way that those who hold them would recognize your description of their views and the chief reasons they give for them. (The more you identify with a particular position, the more difficult and the more important this

becomes.) Helping those in a dispute to better understand others with whom they disagree is in itself an enormous contribution to faithful and fruitful discernment.

(4) If you present your own position on a controversy in your sermon, be explicit about how faithful and reasonable people might think otherwise. Neither the sources of Christian ethics nor moral situations are simple. There are many matters of fact and judgment, many inferences about cause and effect, many decisions about risks and benefits that are possible to get wrong, leading to mistaken conclusions. Thus people of intelligence, good faith, and goodwill may come to different judgments. It is essential that you discuss other views and treat those who hold them with sympathy and respect.

(5) When making an argument based on Scripture or Christian tradition, make it clear that applying ancient sources to contemporary issues relies on many interpretive judgments that might go awry. There are no straight lines between Scripture and House Resolution 2214; no single Christian way of understanding the status of the state or the nature of the family; no one surefire biblical model for faithfulness in matters of money or sex that translates simply to the twenty-first century. When you have done all you can to deal responsibly with text and tradition, and used all the insight you can gain from the tools of reason and the diversity of human experience, you make a judgment and offer it to your sisters and brothers. And then you say, "This is my best wisdom on the matter. But God help me, I could be wrong."[10] Therefore, begin and end all declarations about deeply contested matters with prayer, including the acknowledgment that even our most passionately held views are subject to limitation and error, and pray for God's wisdom and mercy on all.

---

10. This piece of wisdom is paraphrased from Richard B. Hays, recently retired dean of Duke Divinity School, in a public forum about homosexuality recorded at Perkins School of Theology in 1998.

3

Teaching about Moral Issues

Being Good and Thinking Well

In the middle of the nineteenth century, a poet wrote what became an oft-quoted piece of advice to a young girl: "Be good, sweet maid, and let who will be clever."[1] Whether this is good poetry can be debated. What is clear is that (even apart from its implication that being clever is no proper aspiration for a girl), it is not good moral advice. Or to put it more precisely, it does not betray much understanding of what is actually involved in being good. This is hardly an original point. C. S. Lewis observed in 1943 that a person who wished to be good must endeavor to be as clever as possible,[2] but it was recognized as a kind of axiom long before his time. In 1655, Blaise Pascal wrote that "to think well is the essence of morality";[3] two thousand years before him, the classical philosophers had identified ethics as an activity of practical reason,

1. Charles Kingsley, "A Farewell," in *The World's Best Poetry*, ed. Carman Bliss et al. (Philadelphia: John D. Morris and Co., 1904), 5.1 (p. 114).
2. In a pamphlet called "Christian Behavior," later incorporated into C. S. Lewis, *Mere Christianity* (London: Geoffrey Bles, 1952), 41.
3. Quoted in Gustave Masson, *The Life and Writings of Blaise Pascal* (London: Harrow, 1870), 34.

that is to say, a particular application of human intelligence. It is from them, particularly from Aristotle as he comes to us through Thomas Aquinas, that Western Christian thought inherits the central idea that goodness depends upon truth, and truth in turn is founded on a grasp of reality.[4]

Our starting point is a very basic definition of ethics as the activity by which we guide and evaluate action and, by extension, make judgments about character. To do these things, one must know and pay attention to a great many things, including the human context in which action occurs: the structures of mutual reliance that undergird families, communities, and societies. These do much to determine our duties, whether by explicit promises and covenants or by the more informal but essential bonds that unite parents and children, kindred and associates, coworkers and fellow citizens. It is also within this network of relationships, of agreements and expectations and exchanges, that the consequences of our actions must be anticipated and assessed. And finally, it is here that qualities of character like trustworthiness and loyalty are developed and tested, and here that they have their significance in sustaining a good community.

Beyond the social world that is the backdrop for judgments of human action in general, there are a hundred other worlds of knowledge and understanding that must inform morality: all the forms of skill and expertise and practical wisdom that enable one to be a good doctor or pilot, a good engineer or social worker or judge. Such forms of knowledge are part of the equipment for moral life because our performance in these realms also has consequences for other people. Our working lives too are places of the fulfillment or violation of our obligations and arenas in which our character is revealed. All the good intentions in the world will not absolve the physician who harms a patient by failing to perform the examinations, review the test results, or keep

---

4. My formulation is adapted from the compact summary of Thomist scholar Josef Pieper in *The Four Cardinal Virtues* (Notre Dame, IN: University of Notre Dame Press, 1966), 4: "Being precedes truth, and truth, goodness."

abreast of the science that guides clinical decision making. To be a good doctor in the moral sense requires that one take care to be a good doctor in the technical sense as well.

The same obligation to be diligent and informed applies to all who exercise power in the world in whatever arena. This includes all citizens in a democratic polity who participate in decision making by voting, whether on particular initiatives or for the leaders who will make decisions on their behalf. Seen in this light, political decisions are not merely guesses about which candidate or party is most likely to benefit the individual voter. They are decisions about the shape of a good community and judgments about the policies and platforms that will best serve that good. Thus they depend upon an understanding of what is true and what is possible and how best to achieve those things that we can attain only together. C. S. Lewis was right: those who want to be good need to be as clever as they can, for there is a great deal to understand and a great deal to consider if you want to discern, choose, and embody what is good.

In calling moral judgment an activity of practical reason, our intellectual ancestors are identifying it as a form of thinking. Like all forms of thinking, it can be done well or badly. This means there are standards outside the individual thinker for assessing the soundness of the process and its results, as one might evaluate a scientific explanation or a legal argument or a proof in logic. One can ask for evidence of claims of fact or reasons to accept predictions about the consequences of an act. One may inquire into the interpretation of moral authorities or the application of moral rules. In short, moral judgments are called "conclusions" because they are the end of a chain of reasoning, and it is appropriate to ask about the links in that chain.

All of this might seem obvious and unremarkable had it not become routine (almost obligatory in some circles) to talk about moral beliefs as if they were completely private or interior matters, immune in principle from being questioned or asked for defense. "Well, that's my opinion," someone will say, as if that settled the matter. But of course it does not, since the obvious question is, "Why?" Pressed, a person may say, "Everyone is entitled to their own opinion!" This is certainly true if you mean only that no one should be coerced into changing his or her mind (if such a thing is even possible). But it cannot mean that all moral beliefs have equal plausibility, are equally well founded, or have the same claim upon the assent of others. And it surely cannot mean that all (or indeed, any) of them are shielded from inquiry, from questions about the observations, judgments, inferences, and fundamental commitments that provide the reasons why a particular belief is held.

Perhaps the unease about being asked to answer why we hold a particular conviction arises because when we try, we find that many moral beliefs are not so much conclusions we have reached as beliefs we have absorbed from our cultural surroundings, our friends, and our relations. Nothing is wrong with this as a starting point. Indeed, without being given some basic standards and accepted ideas, some way of life in which one is formed from childhood, it is hardly possible to become part of a human community. But there is a difference between the way a young child is taught about right behavior ("In this family, we share our toys / say 'please' / use our words when we are upset," etc.) and the way adults understand and make moral choices or resolve moral differences.

Of course, most of the time even as adults we act according to patterns we do not reflect upon much at all. We pay for our groceries rather than sneak them past the cashier; we tell the stranger the truth about the best route to the train station; we wait our turn in the taxi line; and so on. Such behavior calls for analysis or serious reason-giving only if some unusual circumstances challenge it or some brash newcomer violates the established expectations and wants to know why he shouldn't. Then it *does* become important to know why: to understand what is at stake and what commitments are being lived out in our ordinary morality. But the understanding of what lies beneath our moral norms is important not only because it enables us to make appropriate exceptions for emergencies, to explain our way of life and our expectations to outsiders, or to corral unruly visitors. It is important because, in the absence of this understanding, such standards of behavior lose their hold on us as well. They devolve into mere customs, and under pressure they are likely to collapse.

This does not mean that people must be prepared to rigorously defend their moral commitments all the way back to some universally accepted foundation. (There is lively debate among moral philosophers about whether anyone can really do that, and the majority answer is "no.") In particular, anyone whose moral commitments have some of their basis in religious convictions will find it impossible to offer such a defense. This is not because such morality has no rational foundation but because its final basis is a claim about ultimate reality that escapes the bounds of empirical proof and is unlikely to be accepted by everyone. (For instance, the proofs of God's existence developed by Christian theologians are pretty unpersuasive, even to those who already believe in God.)

What I *am* suggesting is simply that adults should be able to hear and to give reasons for why something is right or wrong, commanded or forbidden—why it should be praised or tolerated or found abhorrent. These reasons must be at least intelligible to others, and those who offer them must be responsive to inquiries about the facts, observations, and predictions on which their particular judgments are based. People need to be prepared to enter into exchanges with others about their convictions and how they make sense, rather than to rely on pure assertion, or worse, to give up on the idea that ethics is a realm of sense-making at all. Otherwise, moral claims are reduced to narrow personal preferences, like expressions of taste. When that happens, publicly enforced moral standards come to seem arbitrary, things imposed by the stronger party upon the weaker party. Debates about issues like abortion or the death penalty are no longer understood as efforts to come to the truth, but merely as power struggles over whose preference wins. American society in the twenty-first century bears many signs of being in just such a condition. Given the present state of public ethical discourse, churches may offer the wider community a significant service by providing training in serious and constructive moral conversation.

Sources and Method in Christian Ethics

From a general case that ethics must be something we think through and something we engage with in company with others, we now turn to the particular character of that work as it might be taken up in Christian congregations. What does it mean, and what would it look like, not only to think about our moral positions and why we hold them but also to think *Christianly* about these things? How would we undertake to do so as a community gathered around a confession of faith, seeking to live it out in the complex and confusing world we share? Here I begin with what I said in chapter 1 about the distinctive sense in which the church must be a moral community in order to retain its identity. There I argued that to be the church, and not merely another voluntary charitable association like the Rotary Club, we must root our common life and decisions in Christianity's central claim: that God has acted in the life, death, and resurrection of Jesus of Nazareth to redeem and reclaim the world as God's own. So the first thing it means to think as a Christian community about moral life is to think theologically.

This may seem more daunting yet, that as a minister you are being asked not merely to be a moral theologian yourself (perhaps without having intended to sign up for that) but also to lead an entire adult congregation in doing moral theology together. But there is simply no way to avoid either of these activities, whether they are done consciously and reflectively or not. Like your life, your leadership in the community is *always* speaking. This remains true even if what it appears to be saying is that Christian faith has nothing to contribute to moral understanding and judgment; that being Christian does not make any real difference in how we live our lives; or that we dare not talk about anything that might create conflict because the bonds between us are too fragile. These are not just undesirable messages but ones that undermine the church's very reason for being, rendering its example void and its proclamation unconvincing.

Fortunately, those who decide to make a virtue of necessity by plunging into the work of nurturing moral conversation in a congregation are not simply left to their own devices. We are the inheritors of a broad and incredibly rich legacy of study and practice. It is the accumulated wisdom of many centuries of faithful women and men seeking to be formed into fitting and persuasive witnesses of God's gracious work in the covenant with Israel and ultimately in Jesus Christ. The fruit of their walk with God comes to us in the history and prayers, the law and the poetry of Scripture, and in the music and liturgy and confessions of tradition. It comes to us as well in the stories handed down, the journals and spirituals and memories told and retold of refugees and slaves, of missionaries and mystics and martyrs, that bestow on us their hard-won knowledge, born of experiences both bitter and sweet. And it comes to us in the architectures of formal thought: in the passionate rhetoric of Augustine and the elegant structure of Thomas Aquinas and the rigorous logic of John Calvin, and in a hundred others. Tools for the work are even to be found in the resources of secular science and philosophy, for if goodness depends on truth and truth on reality, then all windows into what is real are also avenues toward understanding what is good.

Along with shared resources for Christian ethics, we are heirs to a kind of loosely structured method—not a simple, hard-and-fast formula for plugging in questions and popping out answers, but a strategy for drawing upon those resources in ways that respect their character. This is the fruit of learning and study, of sustained inquiry and debate across continents and across generations. It gives us a way to approach our sources of moral insight and guidance that is responsible and informed by history, one that takes ancient sources seriously without forgetting the ways in which the past is indeed "a foreign country."[5]

Along with sensitivity to the past, this broadly accepted approach acknowledges and wrestles with the stubborn complexity and diversity of theological sources. This ranges from the many times, places, and voices of Scripture to the particular insights and commitments of the various families of Christian faith scattered across time and space. The recognition of diversity and the ambiguities it creates also extends to attending to the stories and the experiences of people of faith, listening for what is deeply true and illuminating within all the welter of difference and disparity. Finally, in drawing upon all of these sources we have come to recognize that the tools of reason by which we gather and sort, consider and judge, integrate or revise the materials we receive are themselves doing constructive work. We have learned that what "makes sense" or is seen as "reasonable" depends on views of the world and of human beings that are shaped by culture. Thus reason itself is not singular and fixed but is inflected by time and place.

I am, of course, talking about the strategy, now almost routine, of looking to the sources of Scripture, tradition, reason, and experience for insight and guidance in living a faithful life. Various branches of the church have developed their own characteristic languages for this ordered inquiry. There is the "Wesleyan quadrilateral," often cited by Methodists, a phrase owed to Albert Outler rather than to Wesley himself.[6] Wesley's approach, in turn, was an extension of the "three-legged stool" of Anglican theology,[7] in which Scripture, tradition, and reason are named as sources, and experience is bracketed with tradition. There is also the tradition-based interpretation of Scripture, ordered by reason

5. L. P. Hartley, *The Go-Between* (London: Hamish Hamilton, 1953), 1.

6. Albert Outler, "The Wesleyan Quadrilateral in John Wesley," *Wesleyan Theological Journal* 20 (1985): 8.

7. The three sources are identified by Thomas Hooker in the sixteenth century; the analogy (like Outler's) is a modern convention.

and informed by experience as embodied in the formal teaching of the church; this is the rubric most often appealed to in Roman Catholic moral theology.[8] Important differences of starting point, priority, and weight are embedded in these and other ways of expressing what we are doing when we "do Christian ethics," some of which we will discuss further on. But in the main it is fair to say that the Christian church has agreed upon the necessity of consulting these interlocking and mutually interpreting sources as tools for understanding the shape of Christian life in our own time and place.

There are dissenters, to be sure, people whose theological commitments cause them to call this consensus into question. But most of the time, even those interpreters who (for instance) understand themselves to be doing ethics from Scripture alone, or conversely, based solely on the experience of the oppressed, can be seen to be drawing upon all four sources in some way. This is not an oversight on their part but just a feature of the task. There are no readers of Scripture who are not embedded in a particular cultural and theological context, just as there is no one drawing upon tradition who can avoid using that complex inheritance in ways formed by his or her setting and experience. The meaning of reason is partly determined by the stories and the language we inherit; even firsthand experience is already shaped, selected, and filtered by a framework of ideas and expectations before it is rendered into an account of "what happened." In all these ways, the four sources interpenetrate and influence one another, and so the work of Christian ethics always involves interpreting text and world, self and other, along the way.

What it means to make a Christian community a setting for thinking theologically about faithful life is chiefly to engage its people in a sustained conversation. It is to invite them to read patiently and think hard about Scripture in something beyond

8. E.g., in such pastoral encyclicals as *The Challenge of Peace* and *Justice for All* (Washington, DC: National Conference of Catholic Bishops, 1984 and 1991, respectively).

the fragments they usually hear read in worship.[9] It means taking time to teach some of the history of your tradition, in order that your congregants might have a sympathetic understanding of their own inheritance, the particular gifts and also limitations of the branch of the church that has formed them. It involves keeping yourself apprised of developments in wider worlds of knowledge, so that discoveries in science or anthropology, in human development or economics (and the pressing questions they often raise) might help to inform our judgments about contemporary moral life. And of course it means paying attention to your parishioners' particular experience of faith, as well as drawing them into deeper acquaintance with the experience of other Christians, far away in time or place, whose walk with God might illuminate or challenge their own.

In all of this, your job is not to teach your people *what* to think about complex issues. Your job is to teach them *how* to think about them together, as intelligent creatures who are called to worship God with all their minds, a practice whose aim is that we be transformed "so that [we] may discern what is the will of God—what is good and acceptable and perfect" (Rom. 12:2). To aid in that work, in the next section I offer some general guidelines for drawing upon each of the four accepted sources of Christian ethics in ways that are balanced and responsible. They include information to share, practices to adopt, and pitfalls to avoid as you invite your community to explore the resources of wisdom and insight that have sustained, guided, and reformed the church across the centuries. They also provide a window into how people of good faith and intelligence can come to quite different moral conclusions, even while drawing from the same sources.

9. For this undertaking there are some excellent tools, including the 32-week Disciple Bible Study published by Cokesbury, which draws upon the entire canon and uses both workbooks and video lessons to provide a rich introduction to Scripture. Somewhat more academic but still usable with an adult class is Stephen Fowl and Gregory Jones, *Reading in Communion: Scripture and Ethics in Christian Life* (Grand Rapids: Eerdmans, 1991).

Guidelines for Using Resources Wisely

Scripture

(1) Teach your congregation about the history of the Bible.
Many lifelong believers have very little idea of how the Bible came
to be, the breadth of time and circumstance that attended its
writing, or the layers of tradition that are evident even within
a single book. The purpose here is *not* to "demythologize" the
text[10] by substituting a historical-critical approach for the idea of
revelation or the ascription of authority. It is to help Christians
understand the textured and communal nature of the process by
which its revelation was received and its authority recognized. We
honor Scripture by attending to the book we actually have, not
by treating it as if it were the product of a single inspired writer,
or as if it were written in a time just like ours and addressed to
our questions. A better understanding of the character of our
central book will help us to draw upon it more fittingly to guide
our contemporary lives.

(2) Begin with exegesis. If a passage or a group of them is to
be taken as a source of moral guidance, we must start by understanding it as well as possible in its own historical, social, and
literary setting. The use of Scripture for ethics raises all the questions that should undergird responsible preaching. What do we
know about who is speaking and to whom? What is going on in
the community where this is being written, and what can we know
about the writer's purpose? To what genre does this text belong,
and how does this passage fit into the larger work of which it is
part? What is the theological point or significance of the directly
ethical material? This is not to say that a teacher ought to drag

10. The word as well as the aim is Rudolph Bultmann's; see Bultmann, "The
New Testament and Mythology: The Mythological Element in the Message of the
New Testament and the Problem of Its Reinterpretation," in *The Historical Jesus:
Critical Concepts in Religious Studies*, ed. Craig A. Evans, vol. 1, *The History of
the Quest: Classical Studies and Critical Questions* (New York: Routledge, 2004),
323–59.

his or her students through the fine points of Greek grammar or redaction criticism. It is rather for teachers to prepare diligently so that they can provide the best insight into what these texts meant and why they are important for us to wrestle with.

   (3) Let the texts of Scripture speak in the mode proper to each one. There are many kinds of material that offer moral guidance and instruction. We are affected by the heroes we seek to emulate and the ideals we strive for. Stories and examples shape us, as do the laws we enshrine and the rules we obey. At the center for Christian ethics is the narrative of Christ's coming, his faithful life, his obedient death on the cross, and his vindication through the resurrection. All of these forms can bear powerful and important moral lessons, but they do not all operate in the same way. It is important to respect these differences and not seek to extract rules from poetry, or logical proofs from parables, or ethical principles from historical sagas.

   (4) Take account of all the texts that bear on an issue. If the question is "What does the Bible say about X?" then it is important to reckon with every text that might be directly relevant. This is already an interpretive decision, of course, and it is possible to cast the net more or less widely. The point here is to avoid fastening prematurely upon a single voice or perspective, flattening out the complexity or tensions that may be present in the canonical witness. It is also important to note along the way *how* central or recurrent a particular topic is (or isn't) in Scripture; the relative attention given in the Bible to matters of sexual conduct and the treatment of the poor, for instance, may surprise you.

   (5) Acknowledge and address tensions and conflicts where they arise. While we might prefer that the Bible speak about every issue in a single voice, that is not what we find. Even within a single type of biblical literature (e.g., the legal codes of Leviticus and Deuteronomy) or a single source (e.g., the letters of Paul), there

are significant differences that resist being harmonized away. In some cases, it will be necessary to make a decision about what will most decisively shape our contemporary attitudes, judgments, and conduct.[11] It is better to make a considered argument on textual, historical, or theological grounds than to ignore or edit out the actual diversity of views in the canon.

(6) Deal directly with challenges. These include the differences in social and material context, in scientific knowledge, or in contemporary moral convictions that may make a passage confusing, disturbing, or divisive. This does not in itself prejudge the matter. It may be that our own views are captive to the distortions and corruptions of our culture and need to be confronted and reformed by the Word. (So hold our sisters and brothers in the peace churches regarding the majority Christian acceptance of the necessity of war.) It may be (as discussed in chap. 2) that dramatically altered circumstances require the same purpose or principle be honored in a different manner. But these are matters for candid discussion, for patience and prayer and shared discernment rather than for avoidance or a rush to judgment.

Tradition

(1) Begin with the "Why?" question. Because many people hear the adjective "traditional" as a synonym for conservative, rigid, outdated, irrational, or plain dull, it is necessary to offer a rationale for consulting tradition. Why does the church have a habit of including the dead in our conversations? Broadly, it is to gain the benefit of their collective wisdom. In particular, their different lives and ideas may offer us leverage against the deformities

11. E.g., is it the flat prohibition of divorce in Mark's Gospel (10:11) or the exception for adultery found in Matthew (5:32) or the nuanced pastoral advice of Paul in regard to Christians whose spouses depart (1 Cor. 7:15) that should guide our discernment about divorce and remarriage in the church? For a full treatment of the range of New Testament texts on this issue, see Richard B. Hays, *The Moral Vision of the New Testament* (San Francisco: Harper & Row, 1997), 347–75.

of our own culture and the limitations of our own experiences. It is a truism of linguists that you don't know your own language until you learn another. What is meant is that you don't usually understand that your language even has a structure that can be analyzed and might be important until you encounter another mode of expression with a different structure. In the same way, an encounter with the different and sometimes altogether alien way of thinking of our forebears can teach us to see the artificial obviousness of our own assumptions. Otherwise, we might not even know we are making assumptions but just take ours as the way things are. We learn to see both others and ourselves through this lens.

(2) *Explain how the use of the term "tradition" has changed over time.* Today in the academy we use "tradition" in an essentially neutral way, to mean any distinctive inheritance in theology and liturgy or any coherent and embodied form of Christian faith and community. But historically, and in the sense in which it was named as a source for Christian ethics, tradition referred to something not merely descriptive but normative. It was not just whatever forms happened to develop but what the church was *supposed* to be and do and believe. This understanding is rooted in the origin of the word *traditio*, meaning "what has been handed on." Thus the writer of 2 Timothy speaks of the treasure of the true faith with which Timothy has been entrusted and that he now must hand on to faithful people (2 Tim. 1:13–14; 2:2). The central significance of this process of receiving and handing on becomes clearer when we remember that it precedes and is the origin of the New Testament canon.

(3) *Make clear what it doesn't mean to draw upon a moral tradition.* To receive moral guidance from a tradition does not mean to have inherited a fixed and complete answer to every question, which you can simply look up if you have the right book. It may not even mean to have a fixed and certain answer

to *any* interesting moral question. The conclusions reached by our ancestors about particular questions are part of what we inherit, and they deserve consideration. But Thomas Aquinas, that arch defender of theological tradition, said that the only perfectly certain moral principle is that which is based on the meaning of good: "Good is to be done and evil avoided."[12] It can be stated without exception because it is purely formal, a matter of definition. As soon as it comes down to concrete cases, Thomas Aquinas held, so much depends upon circumstances and matters of judgment that absolute assertions are out of place.[13]

(4) Explain what it does mean. To use tradition as a source of moral insight means to look at the life of faith (and faithful life) from a particular standpoint, from a particular community's location and history and conversation. It means to think in ways shaped by that community's language and experience. This leads one to see certain questions as central and inclines one to certain ways of searching for answers and expressing them. It means to consult voices and perspectives recognized within that community's conversation and perhaps to follow a process accepted by its members for arriving at the truth. (For example, members of the Religious Society of Friends—Quakers—convene a Clearness Committee to join in discernment upon important questions both in the life of the meeting and in individual members' lives.) Traditions exist at different levels of particularity: one can speak of Christian tradition, Western Christian tradition (in contrast to Eastern Orthodoxy), of Catholic or Protestant or Reformed or Radical Reformation tradition. Internal to each of these are several other layers of specificity so that there really are differences between the traditions of faith and practice among Pennsylvania Mennonites and Ohio Mennonites, for instance. Thus it is important to identify which tradition in particular you have in mind.

12. *Summa Theologica* I-II.94.2.
13. "The more we get down to particular cases the more we can be mistaken" (*Summa Theologica* I-II.94.4).

(5) Acknowledge the selective and dangerous nature of the business. Attention to the granular nature of traditions as they are embodied and inhabited leads to another observation to be shared. Traditions are messy and complex, full of tensions and inconsistencies, not at all of a unified character. What is inherited is more often like a patchwork quilt than a single fabric, and any use of tradition for ethics will have to be selective. Indeed, tradition itself is already a selection that is remembered and handed on from a wider history. It can be tempting to edit out those portions of our inheritance that are troubling, distasteful, or downright scandalous. But it is more instructive, as well as more truthful, to tell the whole story with all the insight and sympathy we can, and to draw from it what wisdom and faithfulness we find. (Also, in that process we do well to remember that our descendants are likely to find as much to fault in us as we find to fault in our ancestors.) Decisions about what to embrace and what to leave behind are best made in community and with transparency.

Reason

(1) Start with questions. Because people use the word "reason" in very different ways without realizing it, it is helpful to ask them to think about what they mean by "reason" or "reasonable." On the one hand, it can mean anything from the basic capacity to undertake a purposeful course of action (and thus be shared in some measure with many animals) to the ability to abstract and manipulate symbols associated with mathematics and science. On the other hand, what seems "reasonable" is often what we are used to seeing or believing: the customary behavior and accepted ideas in our own setting or what we would say and do in a given situation. We may not notice all the other elements of culture and socialization that define expected behavior and thus look "reasonable" to us. Getting people to explore the variety of the ideas they have opens the way for a richer understanding of what earlier generations intended by citing reason as a moral source.

(2) Share some of the history of reason. The strategy of appealing to reason as a basis for moral judgment dates back to antiquity, but what people meant by this appeal and what role they thought reason could play have shifted repeatedly over time. Classical philosophers understood the basis of morality to be practical reason, the ability to see what goal should be pursued and to discern the best way to attain it. Early patristic thinkers cited reason chiefly as a tool for the right interpretation of Scripture and tradition, a means of resolving apparent conflicts and discerning the correct application of principles and rules. Later Christian theologians looked for an ultimate foundation for practical moral judgments in theoretical reason, an understanding of truth and being as they existed in God. By the thirteenth century, Thomas Aquinas had crafted a synthesis of classical philosophy and Christian thought in which reason is a tool for understanding the order embedded in the created world. This offered a means of natural revelation of God's purposes that could guide action, a model that continues to exercise influence today. Only relatively recently (in the nineteenth century) has reason come to be identified predominantly with science and social science and with the empirical methods of scientific inquiry. Thus in interpreting theological texts, it is important to ask what the writer means by reason.

(3) Invite critical reflection on the limits of science as means of knowledge. In modern usage, consulting reason as a source for ethics is most commonly understood to mean drawing on the discoveries of science. Natural sciences can teach us about ourselves by showing how the human body operates, how it develops, and how its characteristics are inherited and passed on. Similarly, the social sciences can give us insight into the "soft" aspects of human existence: personality development and emotional life and the functioning of communities and cultures as human artifacts. These fields of study can illuminate questions about how we understand human behavior, how we treat one another, and how we try to shape healthy and peaceful communities.

For all their usefulness, however, these avenues of insight have two limitations we must keep in mind. First, the understanding they offer is always provisional, as new research and new discoveries (and the new theories they call forth) constantly modify earlier understandings. (Compare doctors' child-rearing advice from the 1950s to the counsel of present-day pediatricians.) Second, while natural and social science can be very useful for giving us descriptive knowledge—the *what is* of human beings and communities—by their nature they do not directly address ethical questions: the *what ought to be*. That involves further judgments about how "nature" relates to morality, to the freedom of human beings and the grace of God.

(4) Talk about the difference between the empirical method as a tool of science and empiricism as a theory about knowledge. Science is a highly disciplined form of inquiry that uses a specific method grounded in observation under tightly controlled circumstances. It addresses itself only to questions whose answers can be empirically tested and whose results can be reliably reproduced. Empiricism, by contrast, is a philosophical position about the nature and origin of knowledge. In some more radical forms, it holds that the observations of the senses are the *only* means of knowing anything and conversely that only claims that can be empirically proven have meaning. While all scientists are committed to the empirical methods of science in their work, not all of them are empiricists in the broader philosophical sense. The use of scientific knowledge does not logically require anyone to accept that philosophical position—one itself not subject to empirical proof.

(5) Explain the difference between the material explanations offered by natural science and materialism as a philosophical position about the nature of reality. Because science depends upon processes that can be observed or whose effects can be measured in some way, it offers explanations of events in terms of the behavior

of matter or of the energy into which it can be converted. Thus time and space comprise the field in which science operates, and the reality that falls within its area of investigation is restricted to the material world. This should be distinguished from materialism as a philosophical view, which holds that matter (or its transformation, energy) is the only thing that exists. While natural scientists (and many social scientists as well) confine their theories and hypotheses to the material universe, they need not be philosophical materialists—and many are not. Taking science seriously does not commit anyone to this philosophy.

Experience

(1) Explore the terrain. Drawing upon experience as a resource for Christian ethics sounds straightforward only until you try it. Identify with your congregation the initial questions that arise when experience is used as a source of moral insight. Whose experience is applicable? What kind of experience is relevant? Who is the interpreter of experience? Can interpretations be challenged? How do we move from experience to moral guidance? All of these matters and more become important when issues arise within a community, and it is helpful to have thought about them in advance.

(2) Consider biblical models. Examples of experience used as a resource for theological or moral understanding in Christian thought go all the way back to the New Testament. An appeal to the experience of the reader is a common tactic of Paul, who points to it in arguing against the imposition of the law on gentile communities (Gal. 3:4) and in advising single converts to remain unmarried (1 Cor. 7:28). It is drawn on by other epistle writers as well (James 2:6, 13–16), and such appeals run like a thread through the teaching of Jesus as related in the Gospels (e.g., Matt. 5:46–47; 6:28–29; Mark 2:21–22; Luke 11:11–13). It is noteworthy that in all of these examples what is cited is either experience common to all people or common to the shared experience of a community of faith.

(3) Compare contemporary appeals to experience in moral argument with those of earlier periods. In recent popular appeals to experience in moral discussion, the experience spoken of is often the experience of individuals, whether within the church or outside it. These individuals are taken to be the privileged interpreters of their own experience. Indeed, it is common to deny that any person who does not have the particular experience in question can challenge or even comment upon its meaning or relevance. This is in marked contrast to the use of experience as a source for moral theology by previous generations, including eighteenth-century theologians such as John Wesley and Richard Allen, who formalized experience as a source for Christian ethics. In their work, it is distinctively the experience of the community of faith that is drawn upon. Further, the experience is not general but particularly *religious* experience; it is the wisdom about what is good or edifying for the community, wisdom drawn from their walk with God. Popular appeals to experience also differ markedly from those that inform the various forms of liberationist theology and ethics. There too, the experience in view is the experience of a whole group of people: all who share a social location and the particular kind of marginalization and oppression it engenders. The relevant category of experience for these theologians is the spiritual and political process of liberation. Either communal or individual experience may be illuminating for Christian thought and so may be the experience of those outside the community of faith. But it is important to recognize that these appeals are quite different in their starting point and in their assumptions, and each may call for a specific kind of appraisal.

(4) Talk about the character of experience as always (already) interpreted. It is natural to think of firsthand experience as primary, as a kind of raw information that precedes any interpretation. But we know from the study of perception and memory that there is no such thing as uninterpreted experience, at least not for any

creature with a central nervous system.[14] By the time we are even aware of events, interpretation is well under way. Thus the basic human enterprise of making meaning out of experience is always a complex and multilayered process influenced by a number of factors. These include our ideas and expectations as well as our language. They also include the stories we tell and the categories provided by our community for naming what we have seen, heard, and felt. In all, it is not far off to say that experience is not so much what happens to us as it is the story we tell ourselves about it. For Christians, the story at the center of our faith provides the frame within which we seek to interpret the stories of our individual lives. Likewise, the community to which we turn for help in discernment is an important guide in what we take as the moral insight to be drawn from experience.

(5) Address some of the challenges of using experience as a moral guide, even within the community of faith. Given what has just been said about the complicated and constructive nature of interpreting human experience, it should come as no surprise that this source of insight is as stubbornly diverse as any other. Two people who were present for the same event, especially if it prompted strong emotions, will not necessarily tell the same story about what happened, much less agree about what the event "means." Indeed, in one sense they did not even have the same experience. The problem of reconciling different accounts of experience and its significance for faithful Christian living is perennial. A second, related challenge comes in the question of what

14. In brief: Even at the level of sense organs, information is already organized and edited according to patterns that have proven advantageous for survival. The parts of the cerebral cortex to which sensory input is delivered further organize and select information, removing redundancies and distractions so that we notice what is important. This is all before we get to the matter of understanding what the sensory input means, what is happening, and what we need to do about it. And when the data have been interpreted into an idea about what is going on, there is still the selective business of memory, which stores some aspects of the event but not others, and some events not at all. Both perception and memory are in this sense "constructed."

kind of weight or authority should be given to insights drawn from experience in comparison with other sources of guidance or standards for Christian life. Particular traditions or communities may or may not have a formal position on this question. For those who do, this position may range from giving priority to a particular kind of experience (as do many liberation theologies), to making experience a coordinate source alongside the others, to regarding experience as a lens to aid in the right interpretation of Scripture or tradition but not as a fully independent source of judgment. This is one source of the moral disagreements that divide Christian communities.

(6) Note the gatekeeper role of experience in theology and ethics. Whatever official authority is or is not accorded to experience as a source for moral theology, in truth all sources of insight are inevitably qualified by their ability to make sense and to be persuasive to us. Claims must at least be intelligible in light of our experience to have an influence on us. Scripture or tradition or the arguments of reason must resonate with us and our experience of life and faith in some degree in order to gain our assent.[15] Otherwise, they will not be effective in forming or guiding us morally, no matter what formal method we may adopt.

Strategies for Teaching about Ethics

The preceding lengthy discussion of the complications and nuances of drawing upon the four standard sources may discourage ministers who hope to lead their communities in the sustained conversation we call "doing Christian ethics." I sincerely hope not. Its aim is rather to help them prepare themselves and their people for the nature of that conversation: for the patience and attention

---

15. For a particularly illuminating discussion of this aspect of the role of experience, see Margaret A. Farley, "The Role of Experience in Moral Discernment," in *Christian Ethics: Problems and Prospects*, ed. Lisa Sowle Cahill and James F. Childress (New York: Pilgrim, 1996), 134–51.

needed to hear the Word and the wisdom of our forebears, for all the careful judgments and hard work involved in using reason and learning from experience, and for the humility and charity needed to live with our inevitable failure to achieve consensus on every issue. The challenges of the enterprise invite pastoral leaders to think hard not only about what to teach but also about how.

There are a number of things to consider when planning any kind of educational process, no matter what the topic. The first and most decisive is what exactly you are trying to accomplish. Is your aim to provide background information on a complex issue so that discussion might be better informed? Is it to introduce people to the variety of positions on an unfamiliar issue and the reasons why they are held? Is it to make an argument for a particular position that you believe is soundest? Is it to help people who already have a strongly held viewpoint to understand sympathetically those who hold a different view? Or is it simply to help members of your community engage in Christian ethics as an activity, a process of discussion and discernment about the shape of a faithful life? All of these and several others are legitimate purposes that might be served by teaching. But being clear about your aim will help you make the best decisions about how to design the event or course to achieve it.

The next thing to consider is what group you are trying to reach and what setting you will use to do so. Life situation, education, experience, and social context will all inform what you use and how it is presented. The topics and material that will work best with adolescents may not be best with seniors. Those variables and your purpose will also help you to determine the best place to hold your event. A discussion of the use of money will have a different character held in a local pub on a Friday night than it will in the Sunday school room right after worship. However, the pub is probably not a suitable place for a panel discussion on immigration.

Along with using different materials and settings, there are a dozen different ways to structure a learning experience, and the most familiar one of a single teacher or "expert" presenting material from the front of the room is not always the best. Although this can be an efficient way to transfer information if that is your aim, it is less likely to engage listeners or to draw them into their own critical reflection. It should at least be alternated with other kinds of presentations. Many of these alternatives involve surrendering some control of the teaching event, which can be nerve-racking if the topic is especially delicate or controversial. But much can be done in advance toward establishing a constructive tone for a session you do not personally lead, and one crucial aspect of pastoral leadership is developed over the long term by cultivating an ethos within your community that makes it possible to handle challenging conversations well.

One approach that is rarely seen in churches but that can be very engaging is a dialogue. This can be in a prepared question-and-answer format like an interview, or it can be a conversation in which well-informed views are exchanged and explained. For this format to work well, you need presenters with some degree of comfort in public speaking who are equally knowledgeable and articulate. It is especially important that you not stack the deck, so to speak, by pairing a more skilled or persuasive speaker on one side of an issue with someone who is markedly less so on the other side. In dealing with controversies, particularly those on which your views are known, you want your community to hear and grapple with a strong representative of a different point of view, not with a straw man.

Another alternative already mentioned in passing is the panel discussion, something that can be very effective for offering different kinds of expertise on a complex topic or different perspectives on an issue. (But lots of experience with ineffective panels leads me to caution that this depends heavily on two things: your ability to be very clear about what exactly you want your participants to address, and their willingness to stay on topic and within time limits. Sometimes a skillful moderator can help to keep speakers on track.) Somewhat different is a forum, an event in which two or more speakers present a longer and more formal argument on a topic, usually with substantial time for engaging questions from the listeners. Here the tone of the engagement between the participants is as important as the substance of what they say. If they can present very different conclusions in a way that demonstrates not only mutual respect but an underlying commonality of purpose, they will teach a lesson more significant than whatever positions they defend.[16]

There are also more indirect and creative ways to engage a topic, by using art forms such as films, novels, short stories, plays, dramatic readings from historical sources, or even poetry. (For instance, Mark Twain's "War Prayer" will make even the most committed proponent of just war theory think a little differently about the use of violence to bring about righteous ends.) Stories are powerful and draw us into other ways of seeing an issue than can be provided by instruction or argument. They may enlarge our sympathies and deepen our insights even when they do not change our conclusions.

With any of these means of presentation, especially if the topic is likely to raise strong emotions in your congregation, it is essential that there be time for feedback and an opportunity for participants to express their disagreement or frustration within the community. Otherwise these feelings are likely to come out in ways that give no chance for response or (worse) to drive those who are offended out of the conversation altogether.

If time and circumstance allow, the most fruitful approach to complicated issues, or to topics that have become a lightning rod within your community, is to undertake an extended study of the matter. This gives plenty of time to draw on a variety of informants and to try various ways of engaging members in hearing and thinking about the issue and in speaking and listening to one another. Here again it is important to be clear about the purpose of your study. It need not be to come to consensus. It may be enough

16. An excellent example of this method is "Challenge in the Church," a dialogue on the Bible, theology, and homosexuality held at Perkins School of Theology in 1998; videotape recording is available in the special collections archives at Bridwell Library, Perkins School of Theology, Southern Methodist University, and elsewhere.

to come to understand more deeply what is (and what is not!) at stake in the controversy and to remember that what binds us to one another is what God has done for all of us. It does not depend on our coming to the same conclusion about any issue that is not at the core of our profession of faith in Jesus Christ.

It may seem puzzling that I began by identifying moral teaching as one of the indispensable roles of a minister yet have spent so much of this section talking about handing over the actual teaching to other people or groups. But leadership in a moral community is not the same as being the one who does all the talking. There will be plenty of times when you *are* called upon to explain or to provide background on a topic, to outline various points of view or to offer your own. But much more important than that is the work you do in establishing a safe and open space for engaging together in the challenging work of moral reflection and judgment. Where you look for insight about various topics, how you present other viewpoints, and how you listen to those whose positions differ from your own are all crucial aspects of moral teaching, lessons at least as formative as whatever content you directly offer.

However, it is important to distinguish the sort of "safe space" I am talking about from the way that phrase is sometimes used, particularly in settings of victim advocacy. I do *not* mean creating a space in which people's behavior will be protected from scrutiny or in which their judgments or interpretations (even of their own experience) will always go unchallenged. The church exists partly to call its members to greater holiness of life and conduct, always a matter of the deepest possible challenge. Your office is to draw members of your community into the task of all adult followers of Jesus Christ, which is to discern the path of faithful discipleship. Thus the essential aspect of moral leadership is to teach and to model a process and an attitude that combines seriousness about that work with appropriate humility about getting it right. And with that humility goes charity toward all who come to different judgments, as well as the realization that in a controversy, you (rather than your opponent) might be the one in need of correction.

4

Giving Moral Counsel

A Distinctive—and Contested—Role

People in trouble will often come to a minister for help. They may come for practical assistance with anything from paying the light bill to finding a job. (And pastors are well advised to have modest discretionary funds available to help people in immediate financial difficulty, as well as a ready list of agencies or church volunteers who can connect people with other services they need.) Others come for spiritual guidance when faith is challenged or for emotional support in times of loss, change, or transition. Often they come in deep pain, when the doctor's news is bad and they must prepare to face the mortality we so frequently deny. And sometimes people come with a moral issue that confronts them.

People who come for moral help may be looking for advice, for assistance in reaching a decision, or for confirmation that a decision they have reached is a good one. Other times the problem is not what to do but how to find their way back from past choices they now regret. And at other times people will ask for their pastor's help in following through with a choice they have already made. Depending on the circumstances and the conduct in question, the pastor's role in these situations can range from simple listening and reassurance to proclaiming the sure mercy of God, to offering guidance and support in making wise and faithful decisions. But sometimes this last office will require bringing people up short, telling them that the choice they have made, or the action they now propose, cannot be affirmed or accepted as part of faithful and responsible Christian living. Suddenly one has gone, as the saying has it, "from preaching to meddling." This is not an easy or comfortable talk for either pastor or parishioner.

Of all the things about which soon-to-be seminary graduates and recently ordained ministers express uncertainty, none is a more common focus of anxiety than their readiness to offer pastoral counsel. They have, generally, been through at least one substantial course in pastoral care. There they were likely taught some basic counseling skills and approaches and also to refer community members in need of more in-depth or extended care to professionals with more training. (This is sound advice. Note that following it requires you to compile a list of local therapists and counselors whose training, skills, and areas of expertise you have researched and verified in every new region where you serve.)

Most new or prospective pastors have also done some sort of internship in which (one hopes) they had the opportunity to accompany an experienced minister on a number of pastoral calls. These are usually to the sick or shut-in, the recently bereaved, or those facing other challenges that arise in the ordinary course of human life. But seminary graduates are unlikely to have had much opportunity for supervised practice with one-on-one pastoral counseling sessions with those in moral crisis.[1] Those who are at all reflective about the seriousness and potential risks of such encounters may feel with some justification that they are not fully prepared for that role. Some may choose to seek additional

---

1. There may be such opportunities for those who take one or more units of clinical pastoral education, but these are usually offered in an institutional setting, such as a hospital or clinic, and involve different issues and a general population. They have only limited overlap with pastoral care in a church or other community of faith.

training, whether through seminary or in other settings that offer education in counseling psychology or particular therapeutic methods. This is perfectly appropriate and even laudable. But depending on the context and the approach taken in that further study, it may also be confusing.

The confusion arises because the role of a psychiatrist, psychotherapist, or counseling psychologist is quite different from that of a minister who offers pastoral care. All the former are mental health professionals, people whose training and commitments are oriented toward the emotional and psychological well-being of the individual client or patient before them. There is an operational norm at work, the standard of health. But in the arena of mental and emotional health, that is a fairly broad target, defined practically in terms of functionality and the self-reported satisfaction of the client. A person who can navigate the routine challenges of personal and social life, and who feels contented with that life, is generally deemed sufficiently healthy and well adjusted. At the same time, such an individual may be arrogant and self-absorbed, utterly uninterested in others' welfare, and concerned only with personal advantage. The therapist may regard this as an unfortunate set of attitudes and a limiting set of life goals; however, it is not within his or her purview as a therapist to challenge or correct them. The therapeutic role assumes a stance of neutrality regarding what kind of life is worthwhile or what sort of person one should strive to be.

If a client reports emotional pain or a sense of emptiness, a loss of interest or joy in life, broader questions may come into view, like "What do you think might help you engage in your life with more sense of enjoyment or significance?" This is turn may shed some light on the limits of self-interest as a guiding principle. Still, even here it is the individual's own sense of fulfillment that is the criterion. This value-neutrality is not altogether unlimited. Presumably the therapist who encountered a successful and contented serial killer would still notify the police. But within very broad limits, the role of the mental health professional is to

foster the successful functioning of the individual client and to
facilitate the achievement of whatever aims the client presents.
It is not to offer or commend a particular view of human goodness or well-being.

These characteristics of therapy contrast in significant ways
with the nature and purposes of pastoral care as provided by the
minister of a church or other Christian community.[2] The fundamental question from the viewpoint of pastoral counseling is not
how you as an individual can best obtain whatever you might want
from your life. It is rather how you can take your place within the
body of Christ and become the person God calls and empowers you
to be. Its aims are to equip you for ministry, and ultimately to fit
you for the communion of the saints and the company of heaven.
This will certainly involve bringing attention to your strengths and
weaknesses as well as your personal gifts and inclinations, since all
of these are part of how your particular calling is communicated
and sustained. And ministers can and do offer support and encouragement to people in the pursuit of important life goals. The
difference is that both the goals themselves and how they are to be
pursued come under scrutiny in light of the overarching purpose
of the church, which is to form and equip disciples of Jesus Christ.

None of this can justify a self-righteous attitude on the part of
a pastoral counselor, nor is it meant to suggest a stance of indifference toward the needs or the suffering of struggling human
beings. Any pastor with sense knows all too well the weaknesses
and temptations that beset all would-be disciples, including those
who are ordained. And for those dealing with major life losses or
challenges, the church and its ministers are frequently primary
sources of continuing comfort and care. As known members of a
shared community who occupy multiple roles in relation to their

2. Here I am leaving aside the distinctive role of some chaplains who occupy a
peculiar space, serving simultaneously as representatives of a particular faith tradition
and agents of the secular institutions (hospital, military, police force, etc.) in which
they are embedded. Those whom they serve may have diverse religious commitments or
none at all, and such chaplains cannot assume a shared confessional basis in their work.

parishioners, pastors are much more likely than other caregivers to offer personal emotional support and practical help to those whom they serve as counselors. But they do not, and properly cannot, come to this aspect of their work from a posture of neutrality, nor can they assume a false agnosticism about what is true and important and good. They must come to the counseling session as representatives of the church and bearers of the gospel, for this is their true calling as well as their actual expertise. It is also the source of whatever wisdom and help they have to offer.

But the foregoing can be and is debated, causing some ministers to step back from the role of moral guidance in favor of offering support for the individual's autonomous decisions, whatever they might be. This is due in some part to the influence of models drawn from psychotherapy on education and practice in pastoral counseling. But it is due in even larger part to the shifts in broader intellectual and cultural attitudes toward ethics as a category that I outlined in the previous chapter.[3] In our social context, where moral decisions are regarded more as matters of taste than of judgment, as personal choices that are protected from inquiry as a form of respect for privacy, there is often a great deal of unease about offering moral guidance. And to be fair, some of this unease arises for good reasons. We have seen how charismatic and unscrupulous authority figures (religious or not) can overwhelm and dominate vulnerable people. They can bully people into submission or seduce them into surrendering their freedom of action and judgment in exchange for desperately needed attention or approval. More routinely, leaders and other representatives of social groups can exert undue pressure on their members, upholding unreasonable standards of behavior or simply foreclosing any discussion or challenge to group orthodoxy. We feel instinctively that there is an important boundary that should not be crossed between moral influence and constraint, where the respect due to every human being's ultimate freedom and responsibility is violated.

3. See the section titled "Being Good and Thinking Well."

Nevertheless, the answer cannot be that the church should adopt a stance of complete indifference regarding the moral judgments and choices of its people. Not only is this at odds with its character as a moral community, but it is not clear that total moral neutrality is a possibility for any group of human beings who share their lives in any degree, even in a secular community. At the most basic level, we cannot remain wholly indifferent to the behavior of people whose actions affect us, and we are sometimes affected by the choices of others even in areas we regard as matters of personal morality. For example, all members of a community bear the burdens (far more than merely economic) of children whose fathers are not available to support and nurture them. Thus the fact that a growing proportion of children are born to single mothers affects all of us and puts a vulnerable population at risk. Even intensely personal choices such as those about sex and marriage can be matters of broad impact and legitimate shared concern.

Apart from questions about the effect of moral choices upon others, the idea that individual choices should be privileged to the extent of immunity from challenge or question is not really a neutral position. Instead, it reflects a view of human beings and of their relationship to one another that would have seemed bizarre in most other periods of human history. To detach the *fact* of choice from any process or criteria for evaluating *what* is chosen is to make human freedom arbitrary and irrational, placing the center of human being in will alone. And to extract moral choices from their context in a community and its conversation isolates moral judgment from the network of relationships in which human beings flourish and give meaning to their lives. This is not a refusal to take a position but rather assuming a picture of human existence that rose to prominence only in the nineteenth century. We fail to see it as a particular stance only because we are so accustomed to its presuppositions, which we often take as required for a free society. But this understanding of freedom as protecting moral choices from any reasoned debate or inquiry undercuts the capacity for the meaningful moral discourse that democracy depends on. We see its corrosive effects in the polarized political rhetoric of our day and in the frozen and fruitless character of our public controversies.

The contrast with the basic commitments of Christian faith and the communities gathered around them could hardly be more dramatic. Although that faith honors the capacity for free choice as an aspect of our being made in God's image, it regards moral freedom as not an end in itself so much as a means to a further end. It is not choice as such but rather righteousness that is prized, a standard defined by likeness to the faithfulness, justice, and mercy of God (Gal. 5:1, 13–14). Instead of supposing that moral choices are private matters, Christian tradition assumes that wisdom, counsel, and forgiveness are to be sought in the community through its shared processes of prayer and discernment (James 1:5; 5:16). Far from suggesting that members have a right not to be questioned about their moral behavior, the New Testament insists that we have an obligation to confront one another and to listen when we are confronted in turn (Gal. 6:1–2). We are to seek forgiveness if we have offended (Matt. 5:23–24) and reconciliation when we are the offended party (Matt. 18:15–17, 21–22).

In the work of moral discernment, a key criterion for the judgment of any action is its effect on the community, a standard more important than who is right in a dispute. For example, in addressing a division in the contentious Corinthian church over whether Christians may eat meat sacrificed in pagan rituals, Paul says bluntly, "We know that 'no idol in the world really exists'" (1 Cor. 8:4). This suggests that he sides with those who see no problem with eating whatever is offered in the marketplace. Nevertheless, he counsels those without any qualms of conscience to avoid eating such meat because it might cause scandal or stir temptation in other members of the community. "But when you thus sin against members of your family, and wound their conscience when it is weak, you sin against Christ" (1 Cor. 8:12). The standard for how a Christian should behave is not, "What am I in my freedom allowed to do?" It is, "What will strengthen and build up the body of Christ, particularly its most vulnerable members?" (1 Cor. 6:12; 8:9; 9:1–19).

We have a duty to persuade and counsel, confront and admonish each other when one of us goes astray. In this we seek not our own vindication but the welfare of the brother or sister, the holiness of the church, and the good repute of the gospel (1 Cor. 6:7; 10:23–24, 31–33). It is not for nothing that the church uses the language of family and of the body to describe its character: we are members of one another, united (whether we like it or not) by what God in Christ has done for us. In belonging to God, we also belong to one another and so have a vital interest in each other's moral and spiritual welfare. We cannot adopt the polite indifference of strangers without denying our identity. But in offering moral counsel we come to one another not as sources of authority wielding power. We come simply as those who care for one another and call one another to the true freedom that comes from serving Christ.

Moral Guidance in Community

Leadership as Representation

What we look for within a community shaped by this set of commitments is not an effort to enforce conformity or to discipline external conduct by the threat of punishment. Instead, we expect appeals to conscience: to the needs of our brothers and sisters, to the generosity of Christ, to the example of the saints, and to the demands of our high calling. All of these rest on a claim about the truth and depend on a vision of what life devoted to sharing in God's redeeming work might look like. They are appeals to freedom, not a form of constraint. To be sure, the challenges of such a life are real, and its demands sometimes astonishingly high. So we find in the advice of the Sermon on the Mount to welcome persecution (Matt. 5:11), or in the cheerful counsel in Luke's Gospel to disdain worry about the means of bodily life in favor of single-hearted devotion to the reign of God (Luke 12:29–31). Still, even when framed as imperatives, such calls always retain the character of possibility and invitation. They are grounded in the good news of God's saving love from which nothing can separate us. It is on this basis that disciples are repeatedly told, "Do not be afraid!" and such freedom from fear is expected to enable generous sharing and bold witness and patient endurance (e.g., Matt. 6:25–34; 10:26–31; Luke 12:32; John 14:27). But even these marks of faithfulness are only signs of something greater. In the end, as Paul reminds his contentious community in Corinth (1 Cor. 13), what is decisive is our being formed in the capacity to love as we have been loved. Such a love cannot be required or commanded; it can only be evoked, brought forth by gratitude and delight in the overwhelming goodness of God, formed and empowered by the Holy Spirit.

Framed by this understanding, the role of a pastor in offering moral guidance cannot be regarded as optional, something that can be laid aside when it is socially awkward or out of keeping with the surrounding culture. But neither is it isolated, belonging only to the office of the ordained person as one invested with a form of institutional power. Ministers do not simply present their own personal opinions and advice, nor do they speak from a posture of superior moral wisdom. They represent the Christian community as a whole, not just the particular congregation or institution wherein an individual minister serves but also the body of the church as it endures across history and is dispersed around the globe. The authority and responsibility of a minister is to serve as the bearer of a tradition, both as it is inscribed in the Scripture, creeds, and liturgies of the church over time and as it is embodied (however imperfectly) in living communities of faith and practice. This representative role gives both commonality and distinctiveness to an individual minister's office as a giver of moral guidance.

As we have seen, drawing upon the sources of Christian moral insight, seeing how they relate to one another and to the different circumstances and different worlds in which we must live out faithfulness to the gospel is anything but simple. All ministers will engage the biblical text from their particular location, their personal history, and an ecclesial setting that will shape their reading of Scripture. They will be commissioned according to the practices of some Christian body, appointed to teach and critically engage an ongoing tradition of worship and practice. This will help to define both the pastoral role and the way in which various sources of insight are used and understood. The process of moral reasoning by which general wisdom and standards are applied to illuminate particular cases and circumstances will be shaped by the experience of the community where they serve as well as by their personal experiences of faith, of moral growth and struggle. All of these elements, as well as aspects of ministers' personality and interpersonal skills, will enter into and shape the work of giving guidance. As moral guides, ministers are not *just* single individuals; they are always *also* single individuals, with particular gifts and limitations. Therefore the work of offering moral counsel is something to be approached with care and humility, supported by prayer and wise counsel, in which we remain keenly aware of the failures and blindness that attend even our best efforts. Such a serious undertaking may well be entered into with fear and trembling and in dependence upon the guidance of the Spirit. For all that, it is an aspect of pastoral leadership that cannot responsibly be set aside.

Aspects of Moral Guidance

LISTENING AND INQUIRY

The starting point of serving as a moral guide is not speaking but rather listening. It begins with close attention to the issue as the congregant presents it, but it may not end there. A person in moral distress or confusion may not initially provide a picture of the matter that is clear or complete enough to reveal what is going on or what is at stake in whatever decisions are to be made.

It may therefore be necessary to ask open-ended questions that invite the congregant to share further background of events or relationships and to talk about what seems important to the congregant in the situation. You may find it useful to ask what things make this situation one of moral difficulty or uncertainty for your congregant: what obligations are involved or what consequences the person is concerned to avoid or to bring about. You can ask about what seems clear and certain to this person and about what is confusing or ambiguous. And it may help to provide a wider perspective on the particular issue at hand if you ask the person facing a moral challenge what kind of person he or she hopes to be both in general and through this circumstance. (This may be done by asking people what adjectives others would apply to describe their character, and what are the descriptions they would like to have be true of them.) As the conversation proceeds, it is important to offer back what you are hearing and understanding for confirmation or correction. Many times this will be a person's first effort to put a troubling matter into words, and the work of doing so is itself clarifying. Moreover, it is often a significant relief just to realize that one has been heard.

AFFIRMATION AND SUPPORT

One initial aspect of pastoral moral guidance is affirming the courage and honesty it takes to bring forward a moral concern, especially in a cultural context that discourages people from doing so. It is already an act of faith and faithfulness to seek the counsel and help of another Christian, and in the pastor people turn to the person charged with representing the wisdom of a larger community. Thus it is important to express your willingness to walk with congregants through this situation and your confidence in God's readiness to guide and uphold them in their efforts to live faithfully. Depending on the situation, it may also be appropriate to suggest (with those members' prior permission) other members of the community who have experience with the kind of challenge this individual is confronting, who might be able to provide additional companionship and support. One of the deepest forms of suffering experienced by those facing moral perplexity or temptation in the church is the feeling that they alone have such issues in their lives. The simple realization that others in the community have wrestled with serious problems—violence or addiction in the home, mental illness or criminal behavior, the discovery that a trusted partner has been hiding a secret relationship, or the powerful desire to seek one's own consolation in such a relationship—can break the sense of shame and isolation that keeps people from seeking the help they need.

A Tradition of Discernment

Part of the distinctiveness of pastoral moral counsel is its reliance upon a richly developed set of tools and resources for coming to a resolution regarding the best course of action. There are the time-honored sources of insight upon which we as Christians expect to draw in seeking moral wisdom and the disciplines of prayer and reflection by which we seek the illumination and guidance of the Holy Spirit. There are also the ancient practices of mutual confession, counsel, and support by which we gain strength to renounce what is destructive and embrace the path of life and faithfulness. In all of our seeking, we do not travel alone. We journey in company with other members of the community and with the saints who have gone before, as these are represented by the Scripture and traditions we consult, enriched by the thought and experience of other believers. It is this broad stream of insight we seek to share in the role of moral guide, inviting the one seeking help into a conversation as old as the church about how to live a life worthy of our common calling.

Challenge and Admonition

The role of pastors is to shepherd: to help people remain on the path of faithfulness or to return to it when they have wandered away. Therefore, one aspect of pastoral work is to warn when some act or decision represents a wrong turn and to guide those who have already left the path in pursuit of something they desire back toward the way that will lead them home. This is not to say that the pastor should simply equate his or her own judgment about the best course of action in a situation with the sole allowable decision! In real life, difficult choices arise about which people of intelligence, faith, and goodwill may reach different responsible judgments. The metaphor of a path should not be taken to mean that there is one, and only one, right decision in every matter. Learning to see and to choose more faithfully is the work of a whole lifetime, and some aspects of a lived moral choice can appear only from within.

However, there *are* choices that are clearly wrong. When people choose their own desires over the safety and welfare of others for whom they are responsible, for instance, that cannot be "spun" from bad to good. This is true whether we are talking about the greed of a corporate executive who hides evidence of toxins leaching into the water supply or the blind attachment of a mother who exposes her young children to the abusive behavior of a partner she is unwilling to give up. Each of us has obligations we cannot evade without becoming culpable. Sometimes the personal cost of fulfilling those obligations, of preventing harm to others or simply of acting with integrity when deception is the easier course, can be quite high. In such circumstances, we may need the support of a moral community and the voice of a trustworthy guide saying "do not choose that path." On these occasions, it is the minister's responsibility to name wrongdoing for what it is and to do all that can be done to dissuade a person from choosing a course that will inflict personal harm or do damage to others.

REPENTANCE AND FORGIVENESS

With or without consultation, with or without conscious reflection or even full awareness of what we are doing, all of us make choices that we cannot really defend. We act in ways we know are wrong (or would know if we stopped to think about it), or else we fail to act when action is clearly called for. In the words of the confessional prayer, "We have left undone those things we ought to have done, and we have done those things we ought not to have done." Sometimes this seems almost accidental, as if we were caught off guard and acted on an impulse we regret almost as soon as it's done. For such times, a moment's prayer and a prompt apology may be all that is needed. Other times we walk stubbornly down a road we know can only cause pain in the long run, because there is something we want and cannot let go of, or something we fear and cannot face. The road back from such self-imposed exiles can be long and hard, but once we have gotten ourselves into some far country, that road is also the only way home. One of the most distinctive aspects of pastoral moral guidance is the work of inviting and accompanying people on such homeward journeys. This is the work, both painful and joyful, that the Christian tradition calls repentance.

Here it is important to distinguish repentance, which is a pattern of action, from the cluster of related emotions that arise in connection with our moral experience. Guilt, the inner conviction of having done wrong, is a sense of grief and unease that one feels even if no other person in the world is aware of the wrongdoing. In this way it is different from shame, which is the humiliation we experience when our wrongs are revealed before others. Remorse is the sorrow and regret we may experience over the things that make us feel guilty. All of these are feelings that arise from our judgments of ourselves, which in turn depend to some extent on the judgments of others and the ideas we have taken in from our surroundings.

Such moral emotions are enormously important. They can serve as a spur to right action or a prod to make needed changes in our lives, and a significant part of moral formation is teaching us how to feel in response to good and bad behavior, our own and other people's. It is important to remember, however, that they are not a completely reliable guide. They may be well founded and appropriate, but they may also be misplaced and destructive, which is one of the reasons for seeking moral help and counsel from other faithful people. One can feel acutely guilty without actually having done anything wrong, as one can feel shame even when one is the victim rather than the perpetrator of an offense. (It is altogether common, for instance, for victims of sexual violence to feel both guilt and shame even when they had no fault whatsoever in the matter.) In contrast, it is also perfectly possible for people who are guilty of wrongdoing to experience no sense of guilt or remorse, instead telling themselves a story of how they "had no choice" or were justified in what they did by something that was done to them. We all are more or less experts at such self-justification. And in the extreme case, there are people so emotionally damaged or disturbed as to be incapable of empathy for other beings. They are thus immune from feelings of regret for the harm or suffering they may cause—and are often quite dangerous.

But even moral emotions that are healthy and fitting responses to our own behavior are not ends in themselves. They are only means to the end of rightly ordering our lives. It is important not to confuse feeling guilt, shame, or remorse about something we habitually do with the action of turning our wills and our lives away from the behavior to begin on a new path. It is the difference between being ashamed of your addiction to alcohol and taking the first practical steps toward sobriety, or the difference between feeling guilty about an ongoing extramarital affair and actually ending the relationship.

Ministers can help persons in moral conflict or temptation to be clear and honest with themselves about the difference between remorse and repentance and can help someone to see that chronic guilt is the high price we pay for being unwilling to change our lives when change is called for.[4] They can guide and support persons through the hard and often painful work of recognizing what must

4. Barbara Brown Taylor makes this observation in *Speaking of Sin*, 44.

be let go of and what must be faced in making such a change and offer assurance of the return to wholeness and peace that real repentance can bring. And just as vital, ministers can be on hand to speak the words of forgiveness and the assurance of God's ready welcome, which people cannot speak for themselves, and which each of us at times needs to have spoken over us.

FIDELITY AND CONFIDENTIALITY

Perhaps the most essential requirement of offering moral guidance is a commitment to fidelity. Along with the steady intention to listen carefully, to judge with humility and discretion, and to speak truthfully, guides must be willing to remain present and to work for the best outcome whether or not their counsel is heeded. They may directly challenge some proposed action or express clear disapproval of choices made, but guidance does not take the form of an ultimatum where the penalty for refusing advice is to be cut off and ostracized. Pastoral counsel must always remain an appeal to judgment and to freedom rather than an effort to control another person's behavior from the outside. (From a theological standpoint, a change of action without a change of heart—say, under duress from an authority figure—would not be of much spiritual significance; what a person loves and chooses is more crucial than the observable behavior.) Moral guidance takes its persuasive power from convictions, values, and desires a person already has. It involves encouraging someone to view choices or ways of life in light of personal faith commitments and ultimate desires, including who the person wishes to be. It cannot be the imposition of an alien moral view without losing its character and significance in the life of the Christian community. Members who choose to ignore a pastor's counsel may have taken a wrong path; they are nonetheless part of the community, continuing subjects of the pastor's care and concern, loved and prayed for even if the choices they make cannot be affirmed.

Part of the commitment to fidelity is the protection offered to personal information provided by someone seeking pastoral care.

This is to be held in strict confidence, as something that belongs to the individual entrusting it, and not to the minister. It is not to be shared with any other party except with the counselee's explicit permission. Even when there are good reasons for doing everything in your power to encourage someone to tell the hidden truth or to reveal a secret, there is a great deal of difference between *encouraging* disclosure and *taking matters into your own hands* by revealing without consent what has been given to you in confidence. This is so fundamental a breach of trust that it can have devastating effects on your ability to minister to this person in the future, as well as spreading distrust among any other members who hear of it. This will reduce your ability to help others and to prevent other harms. The damage done in this way usually exceeds any benefit that such forced disclosure may bring.

There are exceptions to this rule, but they are rare and should be carefully and narrowly drawn. It is not enough to believe that some harm might be prevented by your breaking confidence, because it is certain that harm will also be caused by doing so. In some states, ministers fall within the group of "mandated reporters," people who have a legal duty to report direct evidence of abuse of children or other persons incapable of protecting themselves (such as the mentally disabled or elderly and infirm). Pastors and others serving in contexts where they are likely to be confided in should know what law pertains in their location and what specific conditions call for disclosure of confidential information without permission. The general legal standard is that disclosure is required when it is necessary to prevent serious and irreparable harm to a person who cannot be otherwise protected, and the duty to protect is applied with special stringency to vulnerable classes such as children.[5] Even without a legal mandate, should such extreme and unusual circumstances arise, you may judge

5. This standard is drawn from the civil suit of *Tarasoff v. Regents of the University of California*, in which a psychiatric patient whom the doctor was unable to have committed followed through on his threat to kill an ex-girlfriend. The state hospital where he was treated was found negligent in failing to warn the intended victim.

yourself compelled to violate confidentiality as a last resort. But this must be when all other alternatives are exhausted and in the least damaging way you can devise.

Strategies for Moral Guidance

So far I have talked about the range of circumstances in which people may seek some kind of moral guidance from ministers, and I have offered a theological rationale for ministers' being willing to offer it. I have also reviewed the various aspects of that work and the commitments it requires. Now I want to offer a few practical strategies for helping people to think through the moral challenges and decisions they face.[6] Some of these are general and represent a means of helping people sort out the various elements that might be important in making a choice. Others are (frankly) ways to try to persuade people to reconsider a choice they have already made or a proposed action when it seems that it is ill advised or even morally indefensible. (If you remain in ministry very long, you will be surprised by the things people will propose to their pastors.) In addition to being useful in situations where a person has sought counsel or support, some of these approaches may be of help on the occasions when no advice is sought but someone is behaving in ways that harm or scandalize the community, and the pastor finds it necessary to initiate a conversation with the person for the good of the body.

In all of these circumstances, humility, patience, and restraint are required. In your role as minister you can properly ask questions and raise points for consideration that have been left out of an account. You can encourage taking a longer view of possible actions and their consequences than people tend to do when they are in pain or gripped by some compelling desire. You may draw people into deeper reflection about how their choices will affect their reputation and reshape their character. You may even sometimes

---

6. I am indebted to Miles, *Pastor as Moral Guide*, for some of the insights presented in this section.

be called upon to say that what someone has proposed is simply wrong. But short of actual criminal actions, in the end people do get to choose, and your aim is to illuminate their choices, not to take them away. To give moral guidance is to try to help people think more fully and fairly about the decisions that lie before them and to consider what will happen as a result, including how this action will affect the person they become. Nevertheless, the freedom and the responsibility, like the consequences, ultimately belong to the one who chooses. (Though, unfortunately, often enough others must suffer the consequences along with the actor.)

Asking Questions

In chapter 1,[7] I suggested that the practical benefit of some acquaintance with moral theory was that it helped people ask a broader and more complete set of questions about a decision. This is of great value to pastors when they are trying to encourage someone to look at all the dimensions of an important or complicated choice. Each of the three families of ethics gives us insight into some particular aspect of moral life and judgment, framing questions in ways that highlight how all three forms of moral thought can ensure a 360-degree view of the matter and the best chance of seeing all that is involved in a given choice that is faced. This is especially important in situations where a person is afraid or in pain, facing some circumstance where doing what is right may be difficult or costly.

When our desires or our fears press us toward one response to a challenge, we are all strongly tempted to focus only on the factors in our situation that accord with the course we want to take. If telling the truth will be painful or embarrassing, we will be keenly aware of all the negative consequences that weigh against doing so—and perhaps less aware of the sense of unfairness or betrayal we would experience if we were on the receiving end of the lie. If having a clear rule to apply is the easiest and least challenging for us in deciding

---

7. See the section titled "Ethical Theory and Moral Leadership."

how to respond to some church dispute, we may find it hard to pay as much attention as we ought to the unity of the body or the well-being of the most fragile members of the community. If we are attached to a sense of ourselves as easygoing and accommodating to others, we may be slow to see how a steadfast refusal to confront and address some problem in a relationship can be damaging to us and to others in the long run. And when we are in the grip of desire for affirmation and comfort after a long struggle, it will be much easier to see all the happiness we long for in a new relationship than to recognize the seriousness of the marriage vows we took or the suffering we will bring to our children if we choose divorce.

In circumstances like these and a thousand similar ones, questions can lead people to look squarely at the obligations they are under, the consequences for themselves and others if they take a desired action, or the way in which they are deciding not just the present course but also something fundamental about who they want to be. This can help to widen the focus from the immediate moment and the single individual. These must be genuine and open-ended questions, ones that ask people themselves to say what is important about the choice they are contemplating. Ask why truthfulness matters or how lies affect relationships. You may ask what is the most important thing to protect in settling a conflict in the church or how parents should weigh the needs of their children in balance with their own needs and desires. Your aim in all of this is to broaden the frame of reference so that people have a full appreciation for what is involved in the choice they are making. This will not, of course, always bring people to choose wisely or well, but it will give them the best opportunity to see and consider all that is at stake in the decision and to minimize the self-deception that besets all of us under pressure.

ENGAGING THE IMAGINATION

Direct questions engage the mind, asking people to think through all the dimensions of important choices. But our moral lives involve more than thinking. They are shaped by emotions and images, projections and visions of what we hope for and what we fear. And just as people are often selective about which aspects of a choice they pay attention to, they often pick and choose what to admit to the realm of imagination as they look ahead to the aftermath of a complex or weighty decision. Work in guided imagining can help people to recognize and take account of all that is likely to come in the wake of a significant decision, and to reevaluate whether it is truly a path they are prepared to take.

To choose a simple example, suppose you are talking with a congregant who is deciding whether to retire early because of acute dissatisfaction with his job. He is looking eagerly forward to long days of doing whatever he finds appealing in the moment, freed from the necessity to postpone pleasures and interests in favor of work he does not enjoy. By contrast with his present unhappiness, this picture looks altogether rosy. Without aiming to determine the outcome, it can be very useful to ask him to imagine in detail what his day will look like, not in the first week after retirement but perhaps a month or two down the road. When will he rise in the morning? What will he do for breakfast? Whom will he see, talk to, and spend time with in this new freedom? What will he do to engage his mind, his body, his spirit, and how will he pursue the things he cares about? Are there things about his present working life he will be missing at this point? What will he put in their place? What does he have to contribute, and how will he be able to offer it? Invite him to imagine what would be a full and satisfying day for him in this hoped-for future: What challenges and frustrations is he likely to face in realizing his dreams and plans? How will he overcome them? Again, the purpose in all of this is not to change his mind but to encourage a fuller and more balanced use of the imagination so that one does not end up merely trading a present frustration for a fulfillment that is illusory. This might lead to a different decision, but it is just as likely to lead to more careful and realistic preparation so that a worthy future can be realized in fact.

This strategy can be even more vital—and more difficult—when someone is determining a course of action based on an expectation of results that are altogether unlikely, or on so partial a view of the probable outcome that it amounts to a distorted picture of reality. For instance, a single woman admits to you her involvement in a two-year-long affair with a man who is married and has children. She intends to go on with this relationship in the expectation that he will eventually leave his family to be with her, insisting that everything will be fine "once the kids are old enough for him to go."[8] Neither the high risk of that day never coming nor the difficulties and suffering that would accompany it if it did are admitted to her view of her situation. (I am for the moment leaving aside other relevant questions about obligations and character for both participants.) Here, one may try asking her to imagine in detail the conversation between her lover and his wife when (and if) he finally does tell her he is leaving her for another relationship.

The questions that can be raised here are many. What will he say? How will he be feeling about himself as he tells her what he has done and decided? How will his wife feel? How is she likely to respond? Assuming the man remains fixed in his intention, what will he say to their children? How will he explain to them what he is doing? How will they feel? How will their feelings and reactions affect him? How are those children likely to view your congregant and her role in their lives? How will their feelings affect her relationship with this man, given his continued involvement in their lives and his responsibility to support and care for them? Such questions can be multiplied as you invite her to imagine a future of divided holidays and divided loyalties, perhaps not all that different from the leftovers she must accept at present as "the other woman" in his life. All of this remains in the realm of considering the consequences of a moral choice, but since it is often a hoped-for outcome that drives poor choices, this is an

8. This description is adapted from an actual pastoral conversation.

important aspect of moral counsel. Imagining what this course would actually look like may or may not lead her to make a different choice, but at least it places her in a position to make her decision with a fuller view of how it is likely to play out within a complex landscape of relationships.

RAISING THE LONG-TERM VIEW

One way to channel the imagination is to ask people to project two, five, or ten years down the road to all the things they can expect might follow from the course they are contemplating. You can ask questions like: Where will you be then? Who will be in your life? What satisfactions can you anticipate? What regrets might you have? How will you be different as a result of making this choice rather than another? How will the people closest to you be different, or how will their lives be different in two years or five years because of this decision? This exercise seems most natural when we are considering major life choices like entering or ending a covenant relationship, pursuing or changing a vocation, or deciding finally to take the first steps in addressing an addiction. In such situations, we do well to ask what the decisions we make now will mean for our day-to-day lives later and what shape important relationships will take in this imagined new future we are opting for. But it may be a helpful strategy as well for circumstances that have more to do with one's inner life.

The decision to tell or evade the truth in an intimate relationship may be one with repercussions that echo for a lifetime. So may the choice (often hardly recognized as such) to hold on to or to release some long-pent-up anger or bitterness toward another person. Whether to take the risk of forgiving and being reconciled to those you have felt wronged by or to preserve your sense of safety by keeping your distance is a decision with profound import for what kind of person you become and how you live out your faith.

Taking a long-term view means both thinking through the way in which external consequences may build and spread over time and attending to the way in which our choices, when lived out over years, shape and change us from the inside. These effects may alter who we are in ways we may come to prize—or to deeply regret. All the chickens of our actions eventually come home to roost, and we are the home they come to. In matters that touch upon honesty, fidelity, mercy, charity, and integrity, we are not just choosing what to do but who to become. We will be living with the solidifying effects of those choices in our character for the rest of our days, and so will all those closest to us.

ASKING FOR A LETTER

At times it can be very hard to get people facing difficult moral challenges to look at their behavior or their choices from any emotional standpoint but their own. We are, all of us, inclined to pay most attention and give most weight to the aspects of a situation that engage our own feelings and interests directly. This tendency is increased when we are suffering or afraid or when we are gripped by powerful desires. Although we realize that other people will see and experience our actions differently than we do, it can still be hard for the views of others to seem quite as real as our own perspective. When someone in your care has determined a course of action that is likely to cause real harm to others or involves surrendering a commitment that has been core to that person's identity, you can raise the questions, "How will you explain your choices to your family and friends? What will you be able to say that would help and satisfy those who will be hurt or disappointed by your actions?" This is an invitation to see the decision from another vantage point: that of those who are not making a choice but merely suffering the effects of it.

One way to do this is to ask a person whose decision seems unwise, ill considered, or morally irresponsible to write a letter explaining that choice to one of the people likely to be hurt by it. This might be someone directly affected—for example, the spouse left behind if a partner decides to leave a marriage—but it might also be a person who had prized one idea about someone's character, who would be shocked and keenly disappointed at some choice that suggests an entirely different person. It can even be someone loved and admired who has already died but whose good opinion was important to your congregant. In making such a request, you ask them to address what they imagine would be raised as challenges or complaints and to respond to that other person's experience of their decision. Things that seem plausible when you say them to yourself can sound very hollow when offered as justification to a person whom you have hurt by your actions. Actually writing out such a letter can give someone a chance to hear how the rationalizations sound when read out loud as if by someone else and how the reasons look laid out in the broad light of day. In the end, we must all live with the persons we have chosen to become by all the roads we have taken, but it is well if we are brought to see ourselves from another vantage point at crucial turnings along the way. The letter need not be shared with the imagined recipient. The exercise is meant simply to serve as a provocation to deeper reflection, a tool for penetrating the self-absorption that besets all of us when we are in pain.

Conditions and Risks

The strategies suggested for encouraging deeper and broader consideration of important moral decisions will be impossible unless a strong foundation of trust has been established between the minister and the counselee. Even then, if a person's emotions, fears, and desires are deeply invested in a course of action, you should expect resistance if you ask someone to look at what that person has a vested interest in *not* seeing, a selective blindness that afflicts all of us from time to time. The freedom that makes moral guidance possible in the face of such resistance rests upon the minister's steady commitment to the comprehensive welfare of the counselee, a commitment on which the counselee must be able to rely.

Although no one should affirm actions or decisions that are clearly destructive, the minister's care for the person cannot be deflected by dismay or disapproval at whatever actions the counselee has taken or proposed. Nor can the conviction that a decision is wrong lead the minister to act harshly or in a superior manner. We do well to always remember how vulnerable each of us is to temptation and failure, recognizing in every weakness or bad decision we confront in someone else that "there but for the grace of God go I." Here the admonition of Paul is apt: "If anyone is detected in a transgression, you who have received the Spirit should restore such a one in a spirit of gentleness. Take care that you yourselves are not tempted" (Gal. 6:1).

5

Serving as a Moral Example

An Examined Life

Of the many challenges of life in ministry, none is more pervasive, or potentially more wearing, than the sense that you are under constant scrutiny. To begin with, your professional performance is being evaluated with every sermon, class, and public event, not merely by your supervisors in ministry but by every church member or casual visitor. It can seem as if you have two hundred bosses who want different (and incompatible) things from you. Worse yet, not only is how you do your job subject to review but so also is the way you dress, the car you drive, your spouse (if you are married), and the conduct of your children (if you have any). If you live in a parsonage, particularly one adjacent to the church you serve, even the quality of your housekeeping and lawn maintenance may be matters of general observation and comment. Many pastors report feeling that their entire lives must be lived in a fishbowl, and protecting a reasonable degree of privacy for themselves and their families can be an ongoing struggle.

It is a delicate thing to balance pastoral availability with time for respite: to maintain presence and visibility in the community and at the same time to preserve needed private space. This difficulty is not just a matter of personal inconvenience for ministers. The failure to establish time off-duty and out of the spotlight contributes to patterns that are unhealthy both for clergy and for the congregations they serve, leading to burnout or worse.[1] One particular dimension of the "fishbowl" aspect of ministry, the one that is most serious and difficult of all and yet that cannot be avoided, is the role of the minister as a model, a kind of public example of what a follower of Christ is supposed to be and do.

It is a role made more challenging by the tendency of other people, often including those outside the church, to regard ministers as morally set apart and to expect them to be exemplary in their conduct at all times and in all respects. This attitude remains common even among those whose denominational traditions reject the idea of a different moral standard for the ordained and insist on the priesthood of all believers as a matter of doctrine. We may say (and believe) that "all have sinned and fall short of the glory of God" (Rom. 3:23) and affirm that ministers are human beings who stand in need of forgiveness and grace like everyone else. Still, we look to those who lead our communities to live out the gospel they proclaim, and a glaring failure to do so can cast doubt not only on their personal integrity but also on the faith they represent.

What's more, it is not only outright wrongdoing that is in question. Of course, obvious moral failure can discredit Christian ministry in the eyes of outsiders. But even socially acceptable behavior may distort others' understanding of what discipleship looks like if it displays *none* of the distinctiveness that Scripture or tradition calls for in the lives of believers. Onlookers often take a Christian leader's way of life as a standard for what is expected of those who follow Jesus, a benchmark of faithfulness. Thus pastoral example can mislead not only by scandal but also by mere mediocrity and thorough accommodation to the surrounding

---

1. In my companion volume, *Sustaining Ministry*, I return to the importance of appropriate personal boundaries and some strategies for maintaining them.

culture. Ironically, the significance as well as the difficulty of this modeling dimension of the role only increases with the quality and effectiveness of the minister's work in other aspects of ministry. Those who preach with passion and persuasiveness about the transforming power of the Holy Spirit, who teach convincingly about the life of the community of faith as a sign and foretaste of God's reign inaugurated in Christ—they especially will have to give evidence of these realities in their own lives. If they do not, they risk undermining their own credibility and that of the good news they announce. Ministers who take seriously this unavoidable responsibility to practice what they preach can hardly help being a little daunted by it.

But with all of its challenges, the role of the minister as moral exemplar also offers unparalleled opportunities for leadership and witness in a community. Anyone can tire of listening to preaching and teaching about the life of faith (as suggested by the way we use the adjectives "preachy" or "pedantic" to complain about those who seem always to be telling us what to do). This is especially true about the moral aspects of Christian life, in which demands for devotion, forbearance, and sacrifice sometimes seem so impossibly hard to meet that we don't even want to hear about them! But the actual *performance* of goodness, the visible works of those who "do justice, and . . . love kindness, and . . . walk humbly with . . . God" (Mic. 6:8), can hardly fail to be winning, and they offer a lesson more powerful than any words. The pastor who can find patience for the difficult congregant and time to help the stranger in need; the chaplain who has the wisdom and humility to sit silently with a family devastated by grief; the leader of a Christian organization who consistently works to bring out the best in others and generously gives them credit for what is accomplished—all of these not only *proclaim* the goodness of God, but by their conduct help to make it manifest in the world. Because of them, the gospel is easier to believe and easier to hang on to in times of struggle. Their lives are the best evidence of the truth and power of what they say, and thus their lives offer the surest guidance to those they serve.

Unfortunately, even ministers who conscientiously strive to live lives that accord with their proclamation will not always be recognized as doing so. The pathologies that afflict human individuals and groups can infect the church as well. Perhaps the most painful challenge you as clergy may face, and the one most likely to produce the bitterness that can poison ministry, is to be judged unfairly: to have your motives misunderstood, your smallest oversight taken as proof of indifference, or even to have false reports circulated about you, claims that have no basis in fact. Such mistreatment is made immeasurably worse by the fact that it is likely to remain underground. Ill feeling percolates as secret resentment that is harbored but never spoken aloud and addressed. Rumors are spread in whispers out of your hearing, stories told and retold without anyone ever bothering to find out whether they are true. Perversely, conflict that is subterranean rather than open can be more prevalent in churches (where much is made of superficial politeness) than in other settings.

Every pastor is likely to suffer some amount of covert criticism, but when widespread, patterns like these create a toxic environment, one that undermines not only the minister's capacity to lead but also the spiritual health and welfare of the whole community. Perhaps this is why gossip—which we sometimes treat as a minor or even amusing vice, the province of harmless little old ladies— makes the apostle Paul's list of grave sins for which the judgment of God is deserved (Rom. 1:28–32). However, the church remains a community *on its way* to redemption and therefore one in which sin continues to rear its head in the lives of clergy and laity alike. Exposure to criticism, including some that is unwarranted and unjust, comes with the territory of being a visible leader, one who is expected to be exemplary, to become "all things to all people," in Paul's resonant phrase. Preparing to face that eventuality is part of preparing for ministry.

But enduring the unfair blame of others is not the only peril that comes with being taken as the moral leader of a community. There is also the risk of being misjudged in the opposite direction, of being the recipient of undeserved praise and adulation. You may find yourself having attributed to you all sorts of wonderful virtues that you do not in truth possess, at least not in the measure ascribed. This is part of what we mean when we speak of someone being "placed on a pedestal." While it may feel flattering at first, you will find the pedestal an elevated but constricted position, one in which it is impossible to do very much without falling off. Worst of all, if you are not careful, you may be tempted to believe what others say about you, basking in their admiration and setting aside the more balanced judgments of those who know you best, perhaps even the voice of your own conscience. This temptation is, if anything, more dangerous than the bitterness that comes from receiving unjustified criticism.

For all of its pitfalls, the power that is wielded by the minister as a moral example is something it is neither possible nor desirable to set aside. Still, as all the foregoing suggests, it also brings with it certain risks. Serving as a role model is a double-edged sword, bearing the capacity to harm and mislead as well as the power to instruct and inspire. At its best, it offers a picture of what God can do with a committed life, not only in the long-ago world of the Bible but also here and now. The remainder of this chapter will explore some basic insights to navigate by and some practical strategies for minimizing the risks and making all you can of the opportunities that come with the role of "public disciple" that falls to all those who lead congregations or other Christian communities.

Models Made of Clay

Every parent, every teacher, every person who has ever tried to lead and form other human beings knows that nothing we say to those whose behavior we aim to shape is as powerful—for good or ill—as what they see in us. However much we may try to get others to do as we say rather than as we do, the example remains more potent than the lecture. For those who are serious and morally sensitive, keenly aware of their own shortcomings and inconsistencies, this knowledge can be alarming. "What if I don't get it right? What if I make the wrong judgment, say or do the wrong thing? What happens if I have a bad day?" Here the same reassurance given to first-time parents also applies to new ministers: it is the overall pattern that matters, the intention and the earnest desire to do what is best for those in your care that is essential. Getting it right every time is *not* essential, which is a good thing because no one does, not in ministry any more than in parenting.

This is hardly a recommendation of indifference. As a minister, you do need to pay attention. It matters deeply that you realize the distinctive powers and responsibilities that come with your role and that you take these with seriousness. It matters even more that you see your calling as more than a career or an office, but as a claim upon your whole life, a vocation in which who you are becoming is as vital as what you are doing on any given day. But you will fulfill this call well, survive and flourish in it, only as you depend upon the grace of God, understood not merely as pardon but as God's will and power to "bring [the good work begun in you] to completion at the day of Jesus Christ" (Phil. 1:6 RSV). We are all works in progress and so we will remain our whole lives. Part of demonstrating the truth of the gospel is showing what God can do—even with merely us to work with! It is in God we trust, not ourselves. It is only *because* God is the source of goodness in us that God can be the measure of it. Apart from that fact, Jesus's admonition "Be perfect . . . as your heavenly Father is perfect" (Matt. 5:48) would be a counsel of despair.

But since God *is* at work in us, reclaiming and restoring and transforming us so that we may be conformed to God's goodness, we may dare to inhabit even the daunting role of serving as a moral example. We do so in patience and humility, knowing our own deep dependence and our liability to failure. A crucial part of that role is modeling the process of conviction, confession, repentance, and restoration when we find that we have gone wrong in matters great or small. Although some have supposed that Christian leaders should be spared such embarrassing and painful acknowledgments, the importance of a prompt admission of moral failure is increased rather than diminished by the visibility of leadership. It is an opportunity to show that the life of faith depends not on always getting it right but on knowing whom to turn to when we get it wrong and on the willingness to ask for and depend upon forgiveness, both from God and from those whom we have hurt.

My first lesson in this came when I was a new convert at the age of sixteen. The youth minister of the church where I attended was a physically imposing man, well over six feet tall and built like a linebacker. He was also a person of deep biblical knowledge and extensive Christian experience. His was a relaxed and playful personality, not at all formal or severe, but his authority in relation to us was natural and unquestioned. One Saturday afternoon, I attended a Bible study at the home he shared with his wife and their two young boys, and afterward he and some of the guys were playing basketball in the driveway. One of his children, perhaps four years old at the time, got in the path of the play, and his father shouted at him to get out of the way. This caused the boy to turn away, his eyes filling with tears. Immediately the minister stopped the game, and in front of all of us he went over to his small son and got down on one knee, bending his large frame until he could look into the child's face. And with full seriousness he said, "Daddy was wrong to yell at you, and you didn't do anything bad. I am very sorry. Will you please forgive me?" It was a very small thing, and nothing more was said about it at the time. Still, more than forty years later, I remember it as a glimpse of Christian maturity.

So far I have spoken of why being taken as a moral example is unavoidable in ministry and why this aspect of the pastoral role is too valuable to lay aside, even if one could. I have also said a bit about how a person of reasonable self-awareness might approach this role with the right mixture of confidence and humility. Now it is time to talk more expansively, although still quite generally, about what it means to live as an example of Christian discipleship.

Nothing I say will come as a surprise: the answer to how we are to live is at once simple and unfathomably deep. It is also familiar to anyone who has paid any attention in church. The heart of the Christian life consists of imitating the charity shown to us by God in Christ, the outreaching love and active mercy that works to reforge bonds wherever they are broken, even when they are broken by others. This is how we bear witness to the truth and how we testify to what we believe: by making our lives signs that point to the possibility of goodness overcoming evil, whether it is confronted in the form of heated conflict or in the equally death-dealing form of cool indifference.

Seen in this light, the extraordinary demands Jesus makes on his disciples in the teachings recorded in the Gospels—that they think themselves blessed in persecution, forswear contempt for their fellows, forego retaliation, and seek the good even of their enemies—these are not just strange pronouncements, and they are the furthest thing from arbitrary. They are a sketch of what the imitation of divine love looks like in a world still under the dominion of sin. These are the outlines of Jesus's portrait of who God is, the One whose mercy is the foundation of all of our hope. The core of the good news we are commissioned to proclaim is this: that while we were yet enemies, God was pleased to reconcile us to Godself by the death of the Son. In this we learn what love is, and to be a disciple is to be sent out into the world to make that love visible in our conduct.

Of course, none of this is news to us; both the ideas and the language here are drawn directly from Scripture and the traditions of the church. But its very familiarity can make it hard for us to hear with any freshness. It may help if we bring this soaring but abstract account nearer to the ground by talking about the ordinary struggles that mark the life of any concrete Christian community and about the practical implications of taking charity as a working standard to guide ministry. Here, the much-quoted description of love offered in 1 Corinthians 13 is helpfully specific, and to it we turn for guidance.

Love as a Practical Norm

Love Is Patient and Kind

While it is easy to admire patience in others, especially when it is being shown toward us, the truth is that patience is developed only by being tried, which is hardly ever a pleasant experience. It is when listening to the tenth complaint of the parishioner who (still) doesn't like the new organ, or answering the same question asked by the same teacher every quarter about ordering different Sunday school material, or providing the fourth long explanation to the fourth customer service representative about the broken furnace, or sitting through the third unproductive committee meeting of the day—it is here that we struggle to remain present and attentive to the person or persons before us. It is hard work to behave with courtesy and kindness when we are frustrated inside and full of a sense of urgency, thinking about all the important things we might be doing if it weren't for this infernal waste of our time! But the thing we are doing is itself important, for the most basic work of love is simply to pay attention: to reaffirm the worth of all whom we see by truly seeing them for what they are, the human creatures made by God and intended for eternal communion, ones "for whom Christ died," as Paul bluntly reminds us. John Chrysostom once called family life "a school for holiness." I suspect this was not because it was so wonderful but because it was so hard and thus afforded so many opportunities to grow in virtue. He probably would have said the same thing about life in ministry.

Love Is Not Envious

It can seem as if the job of the minister is to do everything—and be good at it. You are supposed to craft beautiful and moving liturgies; write and deliver exegetically sound, edifying, and engaging sermons; and coordinate the contributions of diverse participants in worship. You must guide, oversee, and integrate the work of the numerous volunteers and committees who help to carry out the tasks and ministries of the church. You are to be sure that the proper reports are written, official denominational requirements satisfied, and the books kept in good order. You are ultimately responsible for the programs in Christian education and the spiritual formation of members, as well as for the financial health and viability of the church as an organization. And you are to manage all of this while maintaining warm pastoral relationships with members and friends and devoting much time to study and prayer. If all of this sounds overwhelming, it certainly can be. Therefore, one of the essential forms of skill and wisdom in ministry is the ability to delegate substantial leadership roles to members of the congregation, calling them into service to the community that is the work of all who are baptized.

However, I have been surprised to see how many ministers seem to revel in being at the center of everything and have difficulty letting go of visibility and control in any aspect of the church's work. Instead of receiving with gratitude (and relief!) the abilities of others to bless and enrich the community, they seem to view other potential leaders as threats or challenges and to feel themselves to be in competition with them. This leaves them unable to welcome and appreciate others' gifts, particularly gifts they themselves do not share in equal measure. Thus envy is born of anxiety and insecurity, and it damages both the individuals so dismissed and the community that might be nourished and strengthened by their contributions. But knowing the wealth of God's love makes one strong and not fearful, secure in the worth of being a beloved child and servant of God and so able to rejoice freely in the good gifts given to others, "[glorifying] God, who [has] given such authority to human beings" (Matt. 9:8).

Love Is Not Boastful, Arrogant, or Rude

Anyone who has attended a number of professional gatherings of ministers—conferences, continuing education events, meetings of denominational boards and committees—will recognize the following description. In multiple conversations between new acquaintances or longtime associates, people are catching up with who is in what church or organization and who is moving into positions of greater authority or prominence, the most prestigious pulpits or the most visible offices. This is no doubt inevitable, a means of keeping track of the institutions where ministry is embedded and the colleagues with whom the work is shared. But it is also a kind of benchmarking, a way of comparing your own achievements with others' and marking your position on the ladder of advancement and success. Understandable as this may be, it remains a distraction at best; at worst, it can turn even the service of God into just one more arena of human self-promotion, calling to mind the dispute among the disciples over who was the greatest (Luke 22:24–26).

It is true that effectiveness in ministry requires confidence in your calling and the gifts that equip you for it. But the word "gift" remains key, as Paul reminds his Corinthian congregants, proud over their spiritual accomplishments and fighting for preeminence: "What do you have that you did not receive? And if you received it, why do you boast as if it were not a gift?" (1 Cor. 4:7). Those who live in daily acknowledgment and dependence on the Giver of all gifts need not boast or prove themselves in competition with others who serve the same Lord. Nor will they allow their confidence to shade over into the conviction that they are always right and never in need of counsel or correction. They are able to receive all help with humble gratitude, rejoicing that God is at work in the whole body of the church, bringing to birth what no one of us can do alone.

Love Does Not Insist on Its Own Way

It is hard to let go of the reins: to let a path be chosen that is not the one you would choose or to cooperate with a decision that is not the one you would make. It is especially hard when you have a lively sense of the importance of the tasks at hand and care deeply about the outcome. This aspect of charity is more of a challenge the more deeply you are invested in ministry. But part of the wisdom of leadership is realizing that often something beyond the particular decision is at stake, for others and also possibly for you. It may be a matter of feeling important or trusted or taken seriously. It may be a need for validation of one's judgment or appreciation of one's own labor and commitment. In all of these and other ways, having a decision go the way you favor can seem like vindication—and having it go against your best judgment can feel like a repudiation, a personal rejection. But as one translation renders the text, love "is not self-seeking" (1 Cor. 13:5 NIV).

This is why it is so important that the minister sometimes be the one to yield to the opinions of others. This does not mean that you should misrepresent your own views or betray what really is a matter of principle. There are things that really must be resisted. But many differences of opinion in the church are fueled less by principle than by a very human preference for having things we care about go our way. As a minister, you show leadership by hearing and taking seriously the views of others in the community and also by being willing to be overruled on matters that are not at your sole discretion. This remains the case even when you are sure that you are in the right. After all, you might be wrong about that, and in any event, being right is often not sufficient. Many times the process is every bit as important as the result. A leader wins the right to be trusted partly by trusting others and ultimately by trusting that God is at work even where things do not go as the leader thinks best.

Love Is Not Irritable or Resentful

It is not enough to sullenly acquiesce when a decision has gone against your own judgment. You must be able to genuinely accept the path chosen by the community, to lay down the stake we all have in being right, in order to work graciously with others to bring about the best result. (Otherwise, you have not really given up getting your own way.) In some ways, this may be the hardest test of all, surrendering the internal feelings of grievance or frustration that can simmer under the surface when you regard a course of action as ill advised. But failing to do so, cherishing ill will or resentment toward colleagues or parishioners over some disagreement, is worse than any misjudgment or wrong decision that the disagreement might engender. It is an indulgence in the very same subterranean conflict I spoke of earlier as undermining the church. The health and flourishing of a congregation as a community of witness and service depends upon the maintenance of truthful communication and good faith among leaders and members. That relationship can be broken from either side, but the responsibility to sustain it weighs more heavily on those who have been appointed to lead.

Love Does Not Rejoice in Wrongdoing but Rejoices in the Truth

When I was much younger, I found 1 Corinthians 13:6 perplexing. Why would anyone, loving or not, rejoice in wrongdoing? Despite Jesus's admonition about the blessings of persecution, we surely do not rejoice when we are the victims of others' wrongdoing! And when we ourselves do what is wrong, we are more likely to rationalize or deny it than to rejoice over it. All this wondering was before I had encountered, in others or in myself, the perverse pleasures of feeling righteous by contrast with the poor behavior of other people, like the Pharisee in Jesus's story who prays, "I thank you that I am not like other people: thieves, rogues, adulterers, or even like this tax collector" (Luke 18:11). Those who are deeply honest with themselves are apt to discover some kinship with that Pharisee. But you know how the story ends; it is the tax collector, who dares pray for no more than the mercy needed by a sinner, who goes away reconciled to God. This, then, is what it is to rejoice in the truth: to know and to rest upon the verdict of a holy God that our prized righteousness is an illusion that we may hold before others and even ourselves, but God is not deceived. And so we rejoice in the outreaching mercy of God that is our only hope. It is this that unites us to God in humility and freedom and also to one another, as common recipients of a grace we cannot merit, need not merit, and that will never fail us.

Love Bears, Believes, Hopes, and Endures All Things— and Never Fails

The greatest risk of ministry isn't burnout, though the burdens and isolation of the role can be dangerous and corrosive. Neither is it moral failure in itself, although we have in recent years seen shocking evidence of how widespread and destructive such failures are. The greatest risk is the one that is behind and beneath both exhaustion and much pastoral misconduct. It is cynicism: loss of faith in the meaningfulness and efficacy of the work that ministers do. It is borne of frustration and despair over the high demands and modest successes that are the steady lot of those who remain faithful to the difficult tasks of forming, guiding, and supporting any particular Christian community. This is the greatest danger because it cuts off the tap root that sustains our lives as Christians: trust that the goodness of God wins out despite our limitations and losses, even when (as so often) we do not see the victory.

The demands of ministry go deep. There is a high price to pay in felt helplessness for standing beside those grieving losses we cannot restore, a cost in heartbreak by trying to recall those on a path to self-destruction, drawn by chains of addiction or mental illness we cannot break. There is a price even for struggling time and again to speak the truth of God's love and judgment among the clamoring lies of a culture that promises life in money and all it buys, in power and prestige, or in sex held out as just one more consumable commodity. Fidelity in the face of such challenges must be upheld by the theological virtue of hope. This is neither optimism about the future nor denial about the wounds that mark the present; rather, it is humble confidence in Christ's parting words to his disciples: "In this world you will have trouble. But take heart! I have overcome the world" (John 16:33 NIV). It is critical to understand that it is not *our* love that never fails. It is rather God's love made visible on the cross, which is offered to nourish and sustain us: ever present to fill when we are empty, to hold when our arms are limp, to bless and care for us and those entrusted to our care when all our resources are gone.

Leading through Conflict in the Church

A chapter on the role of the minister as a moral example may seem an odd place to take up the issue of conflict within the community. But here, perhaps more than in any other arena, it is the "how" rather than the "what" of pastoral leadership that is most significant and decisive, and modeling is more important than instructing. When conflicts arise within a Christian community, it matters less what position leaders end up taking on a disputed question than how they frame the question. It is less important whom leaders judge to be in the right in a dispute between members of the congregation (assuming some judgment is required) than how they talk to and about the members involved and whether leaders are able to convene and moderate a conversation among the parties.

Whether it is a matter of strong disagreement about an issue or a course of action, or a personal breach arising from some harm or offense between members, conflict is a kind of pressure cooker. It does not so much *cause* fractures within the community as it reveals them, disclosing in each of us the continuing power of pride and jealousy, anger and distrust, and the ease with which we can subordinate all other considerations to the desire to be (and be shown to be) on the winning side. In this regard, we find ourselves in old if not especially honorable company. Paul laments the fact of his Corinthian congregants taking one another before pagan courts in disputes, suggesting that they might better be wronged than have the scandal of their untransformed conduct on display before the world (1 Cor. 6:1–8).

It is important to underscore that it is not the fact of disagreement or even the existence of mere personal dislike or misunderstandings that challenges our witness or calls our faith into question. These we should expect since it is the nature of the church to be gathered by the Holy Spirit's choosing rather than our own preferences. As Dietrich Bonhoeffer observes in his classic *Life Together*, Christian community exists among those whom we would not choose.[2] What is a matter for lament is our inability to emulate God's patient and steady love toward us in the face of even modest challenges like differences of opinion, personal slights, or minor offenses. The scandal lies in our unwillingness to hear and change when we have caused another hurt or to show forbearance when we feel wronged, despite all the vast forbearance we depend on daily.

The line of the Lord's Prayer we know so well comes to mind: "Forgive us our trespasses, as we forgive those who trespass against us" (cf. Matt. 6:12). That small "as" carries a vast weight of meaning, suggesting that it is our desperate need for forgiveness that makes it possible, but also obligatory, for us to forgive one another. This highlights what is perhaps the central and defining moral requirement of Christian life: that we who live on mercy we cannot possibly deserve must extend that mercy to others or risk being returned to a world of strict recompense, of kept accounts and just retribution, which none of us could bear. So Jesus says in so many words when he tells his disciples, "For if you forgive others their trespasses, your heavenly Father will also forgive you; but if you do not forgive others, neither will your Father forgive your trespasses" (Matt. 6:14–15).

An occasion of conflict, though often painful, is also an occasion to teach and practice (in both senses of that word) what must be key to life in any community of Christ's disciples: the discipline of welcoming one another as companions on the path, joined not by our likes and dislikes, but by the One who calls us on to a shared

---

2. See Dietrich Bonhoeffer, *Life Together* (San Francisco: Harper & Row, 1964), 25–30.

destination. It is God's common call that makes us kin and gives each of us a stake in all the others, whom we meet as those for whom Christ died. And all of this remains the case even when, perhaps *especially* when, we see the fractures in one another, the broken places and blindnesses, the failures of fairness and kindness that plague us all. Rather than thinking (and even saying), "What is the *matter* with you?," we might think, "Ah, there goes another in great need of healing—just like me."

The practical expression of such theological commitments is to be found in the patterns and practices that shape a Christian community's life and work. In their most visible form, these are the structures put in place to discern and fulfill a common calling and the strategies developed to negotiate differences of opinion and judgment within those structures. At this level, the effectiveness of governance within a given community is a matter of two things: first, the clear and transparent allocation of authority and responsibilities and, second, leadership that is broadly shared and reflective of the whole community. But to work well, even the best of such structures depends upon something more fundamental. This is a set of norms and expectations that translate shared convictions into a shared way of life, an *ethos* that shapes how we use and inhabit whatever formal structures are present. In particular, it shapes how we treat the other people who inhabit them with us.

Too often the desire to avoid overt conflict and the equation of Christian love with conventional "being nice" conspire to drive issues in the community's life underground. This would still be a problem even if all parties were able to actually yield their own viewpoints graciously, to accept the judgment of others even when they have reservations, and to keep "no record of wrongs" (1 Cor. 13:5 NIV) when they do not feel treated with all consideration. The problem then would just be that not all members were duly heard and not all aspects of a decision were fully aired. More often, however, there is outward acquiescence but not real acceptance, and offense is taken but not named. In these circumstances, resentment and hurt linger and may manifest themselves in backbiting or deliberate undermining of any course chosen, or in the nursing of personal grudges that can cleave the body of Christ into factions and parties, undercutting its mission and poisoning its witness.

In the face of this, a crucial aspect of the minister's role is to model a way of negotiating conflict that is both straightforward and graceful. The minister must teach but also exemplify what Ephesians calls "speaking the truth in love" (4:15), while at the same time recognizing that anyone's view of the truth always comes from one standpoint. It will often need to be supplemented or corrected by the viewpoints of others, and thus all speaking of a putative "truth" must be matched by genuine listening. In such exchanges, the aim is not to prove a point, much less to win an argument. It is to foster the health and wholeness of the body by bringing about true peace, a peace based on seeking God's wisdom together rather than settling for the seeming peace of suppressed animosities.

Such seeking of real peace will require going to one who has hurt or offended to seek reconciliation in the least obtrusive way possible. In the Gospel of Matthew, Jesus offers a pattern that is at once patient and firm for holding one another accountable in community, always with the aim of restoration (Matt. 18:15–17). Equally, this pattern will call for the leader who comes to realize that she or he has been a cause of offense to actively seek forgiveness and reconciliation, glad of the opportunity to be an example and a sign of our common dependence on mercy.

In cases where deep disagreements persist, when genuine convictions divide a community on matters of conduct or policy and no common conclusion can be reached, two things remain crucial. The first is that each party to the disagreement, having thought and studied, prayed and sought illumination from the Holy Spirit, be able to offer the same kind of caveat recommended to the preacher on contested issues: "This is my best discernment and judgment at this time. Of course, I could be wrong." The second essential thing is that a community constituted by what God in Christ has done for all of its members in common never lose sight of the fact that what joins it is deeper and more central, and incomparably more certain, than the differences of judgment that might divide it.

Markers for Staying on the Path

Life in ministry is certain to bring challenges. Some will arise from the communities you serve, for even healthy communities experience strains in periods of transition, and any human organization must navigate change and transition to stay alive. Others represent the distinctive shape that ordinary life challenges (family issues, financial strains, health crises, the personal losses that are an inevitable aspect of aging) take on when they must be met while one serves in a highly visible role as the leader of a Christian community. The following is some practical guidance for negotiating these challenges with a degree of grace and resiliency, without setting for yourself impossible standards or expecting always to be at the top of your game.

Take Your Bearings from Your Deepest Sense of Call

It is inevitable that you will experience both successes and failures in ministry, some experiments that work well and others that do not. This is especially the case if you try to help communities take new steps in spiritual growth and service. You can also expect to get both positive and negative feedback, both expressions of appreciation and complaints, not to mention lots of advice about what to do differently! While part of leadership is openness to the insights of others, in the end you must pursue the course that seems wisest and most faithful to you, the path you can walk with integrity. In this judgment you are never simply alone: it is entirely appropriate to lean on the wisdom of Scripture and tradition and to seek the counsel of wise and experienced elders. But you will not be able to satisfy everyone, nor can you change direction every time you encounter criticism. You must have a sense of what you in particular are called to do in service to the gospel, a calling that you seek to have continually renewed and refreshed by prayer and study and to which you remain committed.

To speak in more psychological terms, you cannot depend on others' esteem for your basic confidence and self-regard in ministry. Of course, everyone wants to be liked and appreciated, to have one's efforts approved of and well received. Furthermore, no leadership can be successful unless it inspires confidence and commitment on the part of those who are to be led. Therefore, skill at maintaining positive relationships with other people is key to effective ministry, and that requires paying attention to others' responses. But for all of that, you must have a theological and vocational center that does not shift with every congregational vote or every call from a disgruntled committee member. Without such a center, no form of ministry will be sustainable.

Remain Honest with Yourself

Being highly visible in one's work while being held to very high standards of personal and professional conduct tests a person's character. To put it another way, perhaps no form of life presents a more constant temptation to settle for "cleaning up your act" instead of cleaning up your heart than ministry. You must behave patiently when not feeling patient, listen with real attention while being tugged at by other responsibilities, and offer good advice about prayer during periods of your own spiritual dryness. You are called on to preach sermons on texts that proclaim invincible confidence in God at times when you are feeling beleaguered and doubtful, and to counsel couples about the responsibilities of marriage even when experiencing conflict or distance in your own.

To be clear, in such situations this is the right thing to do. Your office as a minister is *not* to offer a report on your own shifting inner landscape but to proclaim the good news of God's love and mercy and to live before others a life that can serve as a sign of that good news. It is not your own faith but the faith of the church you are commissioned to declare, and it is not a statement about yourself but a picture of discipleship you are aiming to offer in your conduct. But in all of this it is crucial that you not lose sight of the truth about your own life, such that you begin to confuse the model you labor to present with the state of your own heart and soul.

There must be a space in which you are resolutely honest with yourself about your own feelings and desires, your struggles with temptation and discouragement, and the wavering of your personal faith—for it is in the nature of human faith to be wavering! You must practice the discipline of being truthful with yourself in order to keep from falling into self-deception and into the dangerous unawareness of your own vulnerabilities that is so often a precursor to pastoral burnout or misconduct. It may be hard to grasp the distinction between trying to behave better—more patiently, charitably, resolutely—than you know yourself to feel on the inside, and simple hypocrisy. However, there is a crucial difference. It is the difference between just wanting to *appear* better than you are and struggling to become better: the distinction between the steady effort to be conformed to Jesus's character inside and out, and merely wearing a false face in order to deceive others. In real life, the development of character is always a matter of being on the way rather than having arrived, and it always includes some aspect of working to shape your own conduct until it becomes, as we say, "second nature." But even as you exercise self-control and labor to behave according to your calling rather than your impulses, you must at least be intending to become what you enact.

Keep Your Own Counselors

Alongside the individual practices of prayer and study that keep you in touch with your life's call, and the steady discipline of honesty with yourself, you will need other human beings: reliable people to whom you can turn for professional guidance, or just for a sounding board when you are uncertain of the best way forward. Depending on your tradition and your context in ministry, some of these may be official supervisors or mentors. Others may be more senior professional colleagues who have proven themselves to be wise and trustworthy. Some may be counselors or friends of long standing who have insight into you personally but who also know the distinctive terrain of life in ministry. What is important is that these are people you can trust to listen, reflect, and respond with care, whether by giving counsel or just by confirming or questioning your own interpretation of events and giving you a perspective from outside the immediate setting of your ministry. This is especially important when a challenge arises in which you are uncertain about what your proper response should be or are in disagreement with other community leaders regarding it. No one is equipped with such perfect objectivity as to serve as sole judge in his or her own case.

Part of the necessity for maintaining trusted external sources of feedback comes from the frequency with which ministers receive unsolicited advice and direction from those within the communities they serve. Sometimes, of course, this is appropriate and helpful, and being able to profit from the insights of others is a critical leadership skill. At other times, however, this feedback will reflect other issues than the ones ostensibly under discussion: long-simmering conflicts between members or very fixed viewpoints about particular matters that cloud the discussion. Unless it involves an intrusion into matters that must be held in confidence, it is usually good to hear out such volunteered advice; very often a sense of being heard and having their viewpoints considered is all such would-be advisors are seeking. A noncommittal "Thank you for sharing your take on this" will be enough. But among the various and often conflicting directives offered to ministers, it is vital to have people to whom you can turn for wise and independent judgment and candid counsel.

Maintain Appropriate Transparency

I have already suggested that ministry calls for discretion about what aspects of your inner life are shared with those whom you serve and under what circumstances. The pulpit, the Sunday school classroom, and the study where you meet to counsel those in need are arenas of your pastoral work; they are not your therapist's office or your best friend's sofa. These are not settings in which to process the crises of your own life and not places to seek to have your deep personal needs met. But this does not mean that you can or should maintain at all times a smooth and polished exterior, pretending that you are somehow exempt from the ordinary ups and downs that mark every individual's life. The changes in mood and emotional state that are part of human variability, the personal and domestic challenges that burden or distract each of us from our work some of the time—these come to ministers as to everyone else. And beyond these, ministers too must know and acknowledge themselves as sinners in need of rescue. The pressures of serving as a moral example are mitigated somewhat by an appropriate degree of candor about your own life. In addition, you will be more believable as a preacher, teacher, and counselor if you acknowledge these facts in a general and appropriate way, one that cannot be mistaken for an appeal for your congregants to reverse roles and become your caretakers.

It can even be helpful to draw upon stories from your life experience, including events that do not show you in the best light or that display your own human vulnerability. The key questions to ask yourself here are, What purpose will this story serve? Does it in some way enhance the exposition of the text before you? Does it help to give vividness and concreteness to a general lesson about a common human tendency? Does it highlight the patient readiness of God to welcome us home when we wander off? Does it share some hard-earned wisdom about the life of faith that might be of use to others? All preachers and teachers of the gospel are interpreting themselves as well as the text, just as they are speaking to a particular community and situation as well as making universal claims about Christian faith; there are times when sharing some of your own story can make those connections plain in ways that enhance your effectiveness. But deciding what to share, how, and with whom calls for careful judgment about the likely effects of the shared information and about your own motives and purposes in making it available. If you feel uneasy about some disclosure, and circumstances allow, this is one of the things about which you might ask an experienced colleague for advice.[3]

Take Time out of the Bowl

We began this chapter talking about the intensely *examined* nature of life in ministry and about the challenges that come with feeling that you are continually being watched and evaluated. I have argued that the power for good that comes from serving as an example of discipleship outweighs the frustrations associated with "fishbowl existence." Still, the stresses are real, and they carry risks: anxiety that may distort your personality and exhaustion that may contribute to burnout or cynicism. It is therefore essential that you (and your family, if you have one) spend some regular and protected time in settings where you are *not* the pastor, not expected to serve as a paragon of all virtues and the picture of faithful discipleship.

This may come in the context of extended vacations, but these are naturally infrequent; to be effective, it is more important that time away from your public office be regular than that it be prolonged. An evening out with bowling buddies in no way associated with your context of ministry may be enough, or a weekend cookout with family friends in another community. The important thing is to be with people to whom you are simply "Bob," not Reverend Smith, or "John and Suzie" and not "the minister and his/her family." It can be remarkably refreshing just to spend a day with people who knew you before you were anyone's pastor, people who may find the idea of you as a minister faintly absurd. Your college roommate, the friend you backpacked through Yellowstone with, the guys you worked with on your first job years before seminary:

---

3. This matter is taken up at greater length in my companion volume, *Sustaining Ministry*, chap. 3.

these people do not naturally see you as exemplary of anything, and they offer you the great gift of not thinking you are anything special. They offer a respite from the 24/7 nature of ministry as a role never completely laid aside.

To be perfectly clear, I am *not* suggesting that your conduct when away from your context of ministry does not matter, as if you could separate your character as a servant of Christ from who you are in your spare time or in nonpastoral relationships with others. You are (like all disciples of Jesus) accountable before God and your sisters and brothers for all of what you do and who you are, whether at home or away, in role or out of it. But in the settings where you are not an official representative of the church, not the person entrusted with the care and guidance of those who are present, you can shed the particular responsibilities of your office in favor of being simply a person, a friend and companion among others. In such contexts, it is fitting to seek care as well as to offer it, to bring your own needs as well as attending to the needs of others. Outside your role as a pastor, relationships have natural patterns of mutual care and mutual disclosure that are the marks of friendship among equals—a possibility that cannot fully be realized between ministers and the people they serve.

Such people can also offer you a needed perspective on the ways in which the demands of the office you inhabit may affect you over time. You do well to pay attention if your oldest friends and the people who know you best begin to say, even half in jest, "Gosh, you're no fun to be around anymore!" or "When did you get so serious about everything?" Of course, it is possible that they are just comparing your fully adult and responsible self to the twenty-year-old "life of the college party" you used to be. But if those to whom you are genuinely close suggest that you are changing in unfortunate ways, becoming rigid or anxious or didactic, unable to "take off the collar," so to speak, this is an indication you should take seriously. It is a sign that you need to find strategies for handing off the stresses that are part of your work, times and places to be rested and nourished as a human being so that you can serve others from a place of wholeness and health. This is not only for your sake, but also for theirs.

The Call to Actual Holiness

We come now to a final observation, one that has been hinted at through most of the foregoing pages, namely, that models and expositions, information and guidelines, coaching and collegial advice—all the things offered and recommended in this text—will not be enough to equip you for serving as a moral example for a community of faith. All of these things together will not suffice for *any* of the aspects of ministry that involve leadership in a moral community, because these are matters not just of knowledge and skill but of character and finally of transformation. It is true that the traits of character we call virtues can be thought of as skills, abilities to discern and to do what is good even when it is difficult. But these are abilities that depend not only on what you know how to do but also deeply on who you are: what you love and are committed to, what you believe and desire and how you conceive of the good. Learning to be just, for example, is not a matter of mastering a curriculum but involves becoming someone who prizes justice above every personal advantage. Therefore, the development of character is the long, slow work of a lifetime.

This much is true even if one speaks only of the natural virtues of prudence, justice, fortitude, and temperance. In the context of ministry, where the powers called upon must extend to the theological virtues of faith, hope, and love, we enter into realms that are literally beyond our power or understanding. As was said before, these are named the "supernatural virtues" for a reason: they are understood to be the gifts and work of the Holy Spirit, part of the inward transformation Christian tradition calls sanctification. Their development means nothing less than becoming holy, conformed to the goodness of God, remade after the model of Jesus Christ into the image of God each of us was created to be. Thus you will need grace to become a minister not just in title and role but in heart and life. And since holiness is a path, not a fixed state, this is always an ongoing journey. You are—we all are—liable to wander from that path in ways small or large from time to time and to find ourselves lost in a forest of confusion or temptation, doubt or despair. Thus another word for "repentance" is "homecoming."

Further Reading

Blodgett, Barbara J. *Lives Entrusted: An Ethic of Trust for Ministry*. Minneapolis: Fortress, 2008.

> An analysis of ethical conduct in ministry that focuses on building appropriate trust within the church community, as well as between ministers and congregants. Morally astute, it offers a nuanced account of the multiple dimensions of ethical practices.

Bush, Joseph E. *Gentle Shepherding: Pastoral Ethics and Leadership*. St. Louis: Chalice, 2006.

> An approach to the ethics of pastoral leadership based on professional ethics, unusually attentive to culture and social context in the dynamics of power.

Grenz, Stanley J., and Roy D. Bell. *Betrayal of Trust: Confronting and Preventing Clergy Sexual Misconduct*. 2nd ed. Grand Rapids: Baker Books, 2001.

> Drawing upon the research done since the scandals of the 1980s and 1990s became widely known, this volume is a good introduction to the topic of clergy sexual abuse, useful to pastors especially for its chapter on prevention.

Gula, Richard M. *Ethics in Pastoral Ministry*. New York: Paulist Press, 1996.

> Recommended for its appropriation of historical professional ethics as grounded in basic moral commitments and for its practical advice about recognizing and managing attraction within a pastor-congregant relationship.

———. *Just Ministry: Professional Ethics for Pastoral Ministers*. New York: Paulist Press, 2010.

> A balanced and thoughtful exploration of the ethics of ministry viewed as both vocation and profession, from a Catholic perspective. Adapts

elements of virtue ethics and the obligations of fiduciaries and brings these to bear on the analysis of perennial issues: power, sexuality, confidence-keeping, and pastoral counsel.

Hamilton, Adam. *Confronting the Controversies: Biblical Perspectives on Controversial Issues.* Rev. ed. Nashville: Abingdon, 2005.

Whether or not the reader is in agreement with the moral methodology or with the positions taken on issues, the book offers a sound and practical model for preaching on controversial topics.

———. *Unleashing the Word: Preaching with Relevance, Purpose, and Passion.* Nashville: Abingdon, 2002.

Offers a guide to effective preaching on moral topics that may be helpful to many. Of particular interest is the chapter titled "Re-Thinking 'Prophetic' Preaching."

Miles, Rebekah L. *The Pastor as Moral Guide.* Minneapolis: Fortress, 1999.

This book is distinctive in that it focuses not chiefly on the ethics that guide the practice of ministry but on the dimensions of pastoral care that include offering moral counsel and even posing a challenge when someone in your care proposes an irresponsible course. Offers concrete strategies for engaging counselees in moral dialogue.

Taylor, Barbara Brown. *Speaking of Sin: The Lost Language of Salvation.* Cambridge, MA: Cowley, 2000.

One might say that this book is not about ethics at all but rather about moral psychology: the importance of how we understand our own actions and the relationship between ourselves and our choices. Taylor argues that the language we use or repudiate shapes our moral and spiritual possibilities.

Trull, Joe E., and James E. Carter. *Ministerial Ethics: Moral Formation for Church Leaders.* Grand Rapids: Baker Academic, 2004.

Chapters are framed as a series of questions regarding alternative understandings of the practice of ministry. As its title suggests, it is aimed at intellectual and moral formation of those in training and includes an extensive discussion of the possible role of codes of ethics as well as several examples in current use.

Willimon, William H. *Calling and Character: Virtues of the Ordained Life.* Nashville: Abingdon, 2000.

Conversational in tone and rich with anecdotes, this volume is based on extensive experience in ministry as well as on the literature of ethics and pastoral practice. Good for provoking discussion among colleagues.

Index